AS/A2 Philosophy of Religion and Religious Ethics for OCR

Study Guide

ROBERT A. BOWIE

$\top$

Published in 2004 by:
Nelson Thornes Ltd
Delta Place
27 Bath Road
CHELTENHAM
GL53 7TH
United Kingdom

04 05 06 07 08 09 / 10 9 8 7 6 5 4 3 2 1

A catalogue record for this book is available from the British Library

ISBN 0 7487 8081 5

Edited by Nicola Haisley
Page make-up by Northern Phototypesetting Co Ltd, Bolton

Printed and bound in Spain by GraphyCems

Contents

Contents

Introduction

This revision guide is for the OCR Religious Studies AS and A2 course, covering all the Philosophy of Religion and Religious Ethics units:

• Philosophy of Religion – Foundation

• Religious Ethics – Foundation

• Philosophy of Religion 1 AS

• Religious Ethics 1 AS

• Philosophy of Religion 2 A2

• Religious Ethics 2 A2

• Synoptic Paper (A2).

It will also be of use to students following AS/A2 level Religious Studies courses on other boards, though students should check their course specifications with their teacher.

Main features

• The book is divided into sections that correspond to the subsections in the specification. Each section starts with a box that sets out what the OCR specification wants you to know about for that topic.

• Each section contains content that summarises precisely the content outlined in the specification.

• Each section has guidance on answering the types of questions that come up at each stage, foundation, AS and A2 where relevant.

• Short glossaries cover important terms and, where relevant, there are key names, works and dates, as well as some critical comments to provoke further thought about the section. You do not need to know these quotes for the OCR exam; they are there to help explain the concepts a little more.

• You will find some text is in boxes – this is to show that this is extra information, which is not required by the OCR specification but which you might find interesting and helpful.

• In this introduction, you will find help on study skills, preparing for exams, and some general tips on answering questions.

How to use this book

• This book can be used as a revision guide to help you prepare for your AS/A2 exams: it would be good to use as a programme for your revision. However, it could also be used throughout your course as a study guide.

- Make sure you revise from the work that you have already studied in class or for homework. This book is intended to back up your work – not to replace it!

- You could use this book as a way of reviewing the course from a different perspective and finding strengths and weaknesses in what you have covered in your class and homework notes.

- The practice questions come with tips for AS and A2 exam answers, not the full answers you will need to give in the exam, of course. You could use them for mind maps (also known as spider diagrams) or full practice answers.

Study skills

Students often find the transition from GCSE to AS challenging. AS/A2 courses place a greater burden on self-organisation and motivation than at GCSE, and the requirements of the course are much more demanding. Here are some suggestions to help you meet these new challenges if you are using this book as a study guide throughout your course.

Making notes

- As part of your studies, you will need to make notes on chapters/handouts that you are given to read during classes. These are important because they will help you to understand the topics, write essays, prepare coursework, and revise for exams.

- Make sure that your notes have clear headings, are dated, and are filed by topic with reference to the book and page you made them from (this makes it easier to go back to the full information again if you need to).

- Important points could be coloured, highlighted or boxed to draw attention to them.

- Your notes may be a list of points with occasional diagrams or could take the form of mind maps, which map out the different ideas using boxes and lines. This approach can help to investigate the ideas behind the topics and allow you to see new points that are being made.

- Review your notes after class and before writing essays.

- If you are given handouts, read them with a highlighter and pen. Highlight the important words and phrases and, if questions arise, write them in the margin and bring them to class next time.

Managing your time

- Plan any free periods, evening and weekend time, a week in advance so you can use them for essential work and not simply what you learned in that day.

- Keep a diary of the tasks that you have to keep up with, the time you think you will need to carry out the tasks, and any deadlines.

- List tasks in order of what you have to do, what you could do, and what you might be able to do, based on the deadlines and time available.

- Word processors can help you be more efficient as they make it easier to alter notes afterwards. Spell check and generally rearrange if necessary.

Create support networks

- Get help from your subject teachers, from tutors and classmates, on how to study.

- Compare your work with classmates and share your strengths: you might have a clearer understanding of a topic than someone else and vice versa.

- Try to identify the strengths others have and think how you can incorporate those strengths into your work.

- If you get into difficulties, let someone know as soon as possible.

- When you get work back from your teacher, make sure you know to what extent your work has met the requirements and where it has not, and how it could be improved in those specific areas.

Read

- Make sure you read what your teacher gives you.

- Read when your brain is fresh, not when it is drowsy.

- Location is important, so find somewhere quiet and light to read.

- If you did not understand something the first time, read it again, perhaps after a short break.

- Try to put what the text means into your own words. You could try to summarise the main points yourself or to a friend – with the book closed! If you cannot recall what the main points were, read it again.

Preparing for and sitting exams

- Know what you will be examined on. Get a copy of the specification (syllabus) from your teacher or from the exam board directly. All exam boards have their specifications on the Internet and you can download them yourself for free, but you must make sure that you download the right specification and know exactly which options you are doing. The OCR web address is www.ocr.org.uk

- Plan a revision schedule. Though there are 168 hours in a week, there will *never* be enough time, so how you manage your time is very important. Divide your week into short periods.

- Draw up a list of all the topics you need to revise and decide when you are going to revise each of them.

- If you have special difficulties with reading or writing, make sure that you ask your teacher about arranging extended time with the exam board well in advance.

- Use different methods of revision. Do not just reread your notes:

  - summarise them

  - turn them into mind maps or posters to stick on your walls

  - put them onto index cards to revise on the bus

  - quiz your classmates.

- Get hold of past exam papers to get an idea of how questions are phrased. OCR ask their questions in a particular way. AS questions are usually divided into two parts: (a) and (b). Part (a) will generally ask you to show what you know about a topic, and part (b) will often then ask you to evaluate the arguments you have written about in part (a) and include your own opinion. The questions are designed like this so you do not need to repeat all the information you wrote in part (a) in your answer to part (b).

- Practise writing timed answers as much as possible before the actual exam. Write your answer by the clock and then look at how you could have done a better job with your notes in front of you.

- Think about when you work best and where you work best. If home is noisy, try your local library.

- Get hold of journals and magazines on philosophy and ethics, such as *Dialogue*, *Philosophy Now* and *The Philosophers' Magazine*. Watch out for philosophy and ethics programmes on radio and TV, such as *The Moral Maze* (BBC Radio 4), *Witness* (Channel 4), *Horizon* and *Hypotheticals* (BBC 2).

- Watch or listen to news programmes, such as *Channel 4 News*, *Newsnight* (BBC 2), the *Today* programme and *PM* (BBC Radio 4), and *Tonight* (ITV), to practise your debating and discussion skills.

At the exam

- Read the instructions and check anything that you are not sure about. Be clear about how many questions you must answer and how long you have to answer them.

- Read through all of the questions in your unit before deciding which you want to answer.

- Read the question at least twice to make sure you understand what the examiner is asking you for. If you are answering a structured question with more than one part, make sure you are confident about each part of the question before making your choice.

- Spend no more than the appropriate time answering each question. If you spend too long on one question, you will not have time to get the most marks out of the other questions.

- Make sure your answer is legible – remember that someone else has to read it.

- Decide on all the questions that you are going to answer – you may think of things connected to other questions as you work on the first one, so jot these down on a piece of paper.

- You may not have time for a detailed essay plan but you can write on the exam paper a brief outline including ideas and thinkers that you are going to mention and perhaps some key terms.

- Answer the question on the paper, not the one that you hoped to see. For example, if you are asked, 'How fair is the claim that abortion is murder?' think to yourself, 'How fair is it? Very fair or not fair at all?' Do not spend all your time explaining what an abortion is and why some people disagree with it without ever tackling whether the claim is fair or not.

- Good answers need not be long but they must stick to the point and answer the full question.

- Go back to the question as you write your answer to make sure that what you are writing is relevant. Imagine the question was not there – would you know what the question was just from reading your answer?

- Treat all religions and viewpoints with respect but acknowledge the differences. Do not be afraid to criticise ideas if you can back up your arguments.

- Do not generalise about beliefs. In particular, avoid 'All Christians believe…', 'All Jews believe…', and so on. There are lively debates within most religions about many aspects of ethics and philosophy.

- Remember to conclude your essay rather than finishing abruptly. In your conclusion, you might refer back to the question and show how you have answered it. For example, 'In conclusion, the claim that abortion is murder appears to be… [*add your view here*].'

Achieving a good grade

- Try and include as much detail as you can in your answer and give specific examples where you can rather than just making general points. Try to be selective about what you include and make sure it is relevant to the question – you do not have to include everything you know just because you have revised it.

- Use the technical ethical and philosophical language and terminology as accurately as you can in your answer.

- Show as much understanding and analysis of the issues studied as you can. For a high grade, it is not enough to regurgitate general points; you must get to the principles underneath them and then test their weaknesses and strengths.

- Try to compare views of scholars and schools of thought and, for a good mark, evaluate them when the question asks for this. Try to make a judgement about the different perspectives – one that you can back up.

- Offer your own personal insights and your own independent thinking. However, this does not mean making bland, opinionated or unsupported critical comments.

- Use forms of evidence to sustain an argument, which in turn should anticipate and counteract views to the contrary. Do not simply list one point of view.

- Try to write as clearly and as well as you can, using your words accurately and carefully.

1.1: Plato and Aristotle

For this exam you need to know about:

- Plato: The analogy of the cave; the concept of the Forms, especially the Form of the Good; the concept of body/soul distinction.

- Aristotle: Ideas about cause and purpose in relation to God; the concept of body/soul distinction.

The analogy of the cave – Plato (c. 429–347 BCE)
The Republic

- Plato believed in two worlds: a physical, unreal world and a spiritual, perfect world. This separation is an important debate in the philosophy of religion.

- The analogy goes that prisoners have been held in a cave since they were children, restrained so they can only look ahead. Behind and higher up, a fire is burning. Between the fire and the prisoners, above them, runs a road, in front of which is a screen. People carry all sorts of things along behind the curtain wall. The prisoners assume that the shadows cast are the real things.

- If one of the prisoners was freed and dragged out, she would see the shadows for what they are. As her eyes adjusted to the light, she would see more and more of the world, including the sun. She would realise that the sun produces seasons and warmth, controlling everything in the visible world.

- Plato argued that our sight reveals the world of shadows, but if we ascend into the upper world, we will see the true reality. Ultimately we will see the Form of the Good, which is responsible for whatever is right and valuable in anything.

- Most people are imprisoned by their misperception that the shadows are the true world. The shadows (the objects we see around us) are poor reflections of true reality – the Forms.

- The cave is the world as we see it, a distortion of the truth. It is distorted by our refusal or inability to pursue philosophically the journey to truth. The journey out of the cave is the sometimes difficult philosophical journey to truth. When those who have seen the truth return to persuade others, they think the others are fools due to their restricted perceptions.

Plato's Forms

- Plato believed true reality existed beyond normal perceptions of the world. What we perceive around us is a shadow of this truth. This 'other world' was inhabited by the Forms, such as justice, goodness and beauty. Forms such as colours participate in the objects around us.

- We might find a piece of music beautiful, or the way a mother holds her baby. Beauty is participating (meaning 'is present') in these things, but beauty itself is beyond our normal perception.

- Protagoras (c. 490–c. 420 BCE) thought you could only ask, 'What is good for you?' But Plato thought you could ask, 'What is goodness itself?' Goodness itself was the highest form of reality, an objective or absolute thing that existed eternally, beyond our limited world. Plato was an absolutist.

- Forms could not have made such a distorted world. Plato believed in a demiurge (a creator God) who took the chaotic pre-existent matter and space and gave it geometric shapes.

- The demiurge used the eternal world of the Forms as a plan for the matter. The demiurge is not a Form, though like the Forms the demiurge is eternal and causes the cyclical motion of the heavens.

- Forms and their perceptions seem only accessible to the highly educated philosophers, leaving many ordinary people cut off from truth. They exist beyond the physical world, so cannot be empirically proven to exist or not exist.

- Plato relies heavily on human mental ability to escape the shadows.

Body/soul distinction

- Plato believed the soul existed before the body.

- Humans remember things from a previous life before that of the body, such as our ability to recognise equality in numbers, for example, two pieces of wood. We also recognise goodness itself and beauty itself.

- Before taking on the body, the soul existed and was aware of the Forms, or pure essences.

- After death, the soul leaves the body and lives on in a cycle of life and death and life. The soul is closer to the Forms than the body as it is incorruptible and eternal.

- The philosopher's soul lives on after the body, immortal and in a state of bliss and wisdom. The souls of those focused on bodily demands are reborn as lower creatures.

- Plato held that the true philosopher should strive to free herself or himself from physical slavery. The mind must be separated from the body and the distortions of pain and pleasure that come from it.

- True reality can only be known through pure thought and the body prevents this. Truth, beauty and goodness are not found in the sensory world. The philosopher must seek them unhindered by bodily distractions.

- The body's weaknesses distract the philosopher. It is an obstacle to the attainment of true knowledge.

- 'The body's need for nourishment involves us in endless troubles…Engulfed in such troubles, we have no time for philosophy…If we are to have clear knowledge of anything, we must be liberated from the body and contemplate things with the soul alone.' (Plato)

- The philosopher's life is the quest for truth; a separation from the body so that he or she may clearly perceive reality. This is the journey from the cave.

- The soul perceives the Forms once it is freed from the pleasure and pains of the body.

- Plato's separation of body and soul goes against the holistic view that self is formed by physicality as well as the spiritual dimension.

- Plato's negativity to the body denies an important element of human nature.

- There is no empirical way of proving or disproving the soul's immortality.

Aristotle on the Forms

- Aristotle agreed with Plato that the Forms were the object of rational thought but felt there was no proof that they existed beyond this world.

- Forms do not say much about the world we live in, they point beyond it, and they do not explain the movement of things.

- Aristotle believed Forms could not exist as things in themselves beyond this world but only as part of the things in the world. They are not objective universals.

- The Form is involved in matter and expresses itself through matter, which has a purpose. It has an objective sense through the substance it exists in, for example, there is

Names and works

Aristotle, *De Anima*, *Metaphysics*, *Nicomachean Ethics*, (4th century BCE)

Plato, *The Republic* (4th century BCE)

Glossary

Demiurge The eternal God that created the universe out of pre-existing matter.

Unmoved Mover Aristotle's final cause behind everything.

The Form of the Good The highest of all the Forms, which participates in all moral activity and good things.

Forms Plato's absolutes, which are timeless, eternal truths, existing beyond this world but participating in it. Aristotle believed they only existed within the objects.

Shadows The things we see that most people believe to be real but which are in fact only reflections of the Forms.

Soul For Plato it is the immortal, eternal aspect of human life, which is close to the Forms and perceives them once it is free from the material needs of the body. For Aristotle it is the character of the body, which lives and dies with the body.

an idea of 'horse', which expresses itself through horses and gains some degree of objectivity through that expression.

Ideas about cause and purpose in relation to God – Aristotle (c. 435–350 BCE)
Metaphysics Book 12

- Objects change in a number of ways and those changes are caused: nature does not act without a purpose.
- If there is any change in the universe, there must be something that initiated the change.
- The final cause behind everything is the Unmoved Mover, which is a pure immaterial being or pure immaterial thought; self-subsistent and self-contained.
- The Unmoved Mover is intelligence or thought. Aristotle never talked about God in personal terms or in anthropomorphic terms as the Greek Gods were described.
- God has no divine plan and does not know the world.
- Aristotle does not explain where the matter for the world came from. Was it caused too?
- There is a disparity between an entity powerful enough to set the universe in motion but unable to know it.

The body/soul distinction – Aristotle
De Anima Book 1

- Objects in the world are either alive or inanimate. All living things have souls that vary in their complexity according to the level of life.
- The soul provides the power of nutrition, perception, movement and thought.
- The soul is not made up of physical tissue but a set of powers or faculties, such as a skill, therefore it is pointless to talk about a distinction or separation of the soul from the body.
- Souls are a part of living bodies and cannot live apart from a body any more than skills can be apart from living skilled people. Therefore a soul cannot exist before life or after it, as Plato believed.
- Souls do not drift into a body at a certain point as they cannot exist beyond it.

- However, Aristotle suggests that a certain type of thought (active intellect) comes from outside the body and is unconnected with the body and separable from it. Once separated, it is immortal and eternal.

Tips for AS exam questions (Foundation Paper)

(a) Explain what Plato meant by 'Forms'.

- Explain the Forms with reference to the analogy of the cave (especially the shadows), but do not get overly descriptive.

- You could emphasise the nature of the Forms, beyond this world, and their involvement in this world using examples.

- You could explain how someone might get to perceive the Forms with reference to the analogy of the cave.

(b) 'Plato's theory of the Forms is of little use.' Discuss.

- Plato's emphasis is on the 'real' world and not the physical world, which is unimportant. Do you agree that the physical world is just a distraction from the 'real' world of Plato's theory?

- Perhaps Plato is interested in living truthfully in the physical world, giving the spiritual world as the measure by which the physical world is judged.

Critical comments

Frederick Copleston (1907–94) explains Plato's view that we could perceive truth through our mind: 'Plato meant to establish ascertained truth. He firmly held that we can, and do, apprehend essences in thought, and he firmly held that these essences were not purely subjective creations of the human mind…Reality can be known and reality is rational; what cannot be known is not rational, and what is not fully real is not fully rational.' (Copleston)

Bertrand Russell (1872–1970) explains Aristotle's views on the relation between humanity and the divine, saying that, for Aristotle, people could only share part of the divine nature while they were living, rational beings. This seems to rule out belief in life with God after death. 'It does not appear that Aristotle believed in personal immortality in the sense that it was taught by Plato and afterwards by Christianity. He believed only that, in so far as men are rational, they partake in the divine, which is immortal. It is open to man to increase the element of the divine in his nature, and to do so is the highest virtue. But if he succeeded completely, he would have ceased to exist as a separate person.' (Russell)

For the exam you need to know about:

- The concept of God as creator: Genesis 1–3
- The goodness of God: Exodus 20
- God's activity in the world and the concept of miracle: Joshua 10.1–15

The concept of God as creator: Genesis 1–3

- Many believe that God created the universe out of nothing – '*creatio ex nihilo*'. Creator is distinguished from creation. God has authority over the world, including humans, and humans have a duty to care for the world that is God's. Creation is good as it is made by God, although human sin may misuse creation or even worship aspects of creation.

- The world comes from God, as light comes from the sun. There is a clear link between God and creation. However, this idea does not suggest a personal God.

- God is described as a builder who constructs the world (for example, Psalm 127), conveying ideas of planning, decision and deliberate act. The idea of God as an artist or builder contrasts with the Greek idea of God as some kind of force or concept incapable of involvement with the physical world. However, the idea of God as a builder also suggests that God made the universe out of pre-existing matter, not *ex nihilo* (out of nothing).

- God is present in the world: God communicates with people in the world, for example, with Moses.

- God's power or nature is described in terms of omnipotence, meaning all-powerful. But God is not thought of in terms of being able to do the logically impossible (such as making a square a circle).

- God is omniscient. God knows all that was, is and will be. You cannot hide from God and God's knowledge reaches motives, feelings and thoughts. God is omnipresent: everywhere, not limited to certain temples or just able to go to certain places. You do not have to go to a physical place to meet God.

- However, how does this explain the natural disasters that cause so much suffering in the world? Could God not have made a better world without such things? Why has God allowed such terrible evil to exist, like mass murderers, for example? Is God responsible for their existence as the creator of all?

- Traditionally, Christians have believed that God gave humans free will to choose how to act, although God wants them to do good. Some suggest that without any evil, good would be meaningless, and that suffering enables human growth.

The goodness of God: Exodus 20

- The Bible describes God as perfectly good and never having done anything wrong. God is the Supreme Good and as God is the creator of all that exists, the creatures derive their goodness from God.

- God is the source of human ethics or goodness. God is involved in the goodness in humans, both in thought and action. God is described in the Bible as love and where there is love, there is God. God is perfectly dependable and is to be relied upon in times of trouble.

- God saves the Israelites from Egyptian slavery and punishes those who do wrong. God is gracious and full of compassion: slow to anger and great in mercy. God forgives and forgives again. The Bible shows the people of Israel as constantly drifting away from God.

- Does goodness come from God? Does God make goodness or agree with it? Is goodness a separate thing from God and, if so, what sort of thing is it? Could God have given out commandments that opposed the ones given to Moses?

- God is law-giver in the sense that God determines ethical codes. The Bible describes rightness and wrongness as God's decision, expressed through the prophets, commandments, and so on.

- Divine judgement is an act of God through which the destiny of rational creatures is determined.

God's activity in the world and the concept of miracle: Joshua 10.1–15

- God acts in the world. God brought about the flood and destroyed Sodom and Gomorrah; God caused miracles to happen. 'Miracles' refers to things that break the laws of nature, such as raising someone from the dead.

- A miracle may be defined as an extraordinary act – above, contrary to, and outside nature, or simply an event that cannot easily be explained. It may be a supernatural act. Many Christians believe only God can perform miracles.

- The Scottish philosopher David Hume (1711–76) called a miracle 'a transgression of a law of nature by a particular volition of the deity'.

- Hume argued that it is more reasonable to believe that miracles do not happen than that they do; to believe that someone has made a mistake or has lied. Miracles do not happen in the present, he said, so accounts of them in the past are probably people making a mistake or not giving a true account.

- Modern science has explained many things today that would have seemed like miracles in the past: perhaps all miracles can be explained as natural?

- In Joshua 10.1–15, God helps Joshua to defeat the five kings of the Amorites and stopped the sun prolonging the day. This miracle goes against laws of nature and shows God to be prepared to intervene directly rather than leaving them to unfold unaffected.

- This raises questions about when God chooses to act and why, in certain circumstances. Why does God intervene in localised disputes in or around Israel but not elsewhere? Why does God not intervene in times of terrible suffering? Perhaps God does intervene but in ways we cannot detect.

- Miracles are sometimes explained in other ways. Jesus may have actually healed people using medicine or knowledge rather than divine power. Miracles may be given metaphorical meanings such as Jesus calming the storm of people's lives, rather than an actual storm. However, this would suggest that God is unable or unwilling to act in the world.

Tips for AS exam questions (Foundation Paper)

(a) Explain what is meant in the Bible by the phrase 'God is good'.

- Make sure you relate your answer directly and specifically to the Bible.

- You could refer to the different ways in which God can be said to be good. God punishes those who sin, making the world a better place for those who are good. God saves those who ask for God's help and forgives those who ask for forgiveness. God sets the standards of right and wrong by giving laws. God is not just goodness itself, the standard by which human goodness can be measured, but is also concerned with human morality and cares whether humans do right or wrong.

Glossary

Creatio ex nihilo Creation out of nothing.

Miracle A wonder, caused by God, which goes against the laws of nature.

(b) 'It is difficult to believe in a God who is perfectly good.' Discuss.

- One good approach would be to focus your discussion on two aspects – the existence of suffering and the existence of evil.

- If God is perfectly good, why did God create a world in which suffering occurs because of natural causes?

- Is this the only world that could be made and are the volatile aspects of the world (earthquakes, volcanoes, and so on) necessary for it to exist?

- You might consider that God is responsible for making human beings who freely do appallingly wicked acts.

- One response to this argument is that while God has the capacity to do anything and creates free creatures who might do wrong, God is perfectly good and so would never do wrong. God loves life and wants life to choose good freely. God is not a dictator that creates only mindless automatons.

Critical comments

Copleston defines Plato's idea of God, as opposed to the biblical idea: 'Moreover, for Plato, God is constantly operative in the world, striving to realise the ideal in the concrete and actual world...He is the Reason, Divine Providence, operative in the cosmos.' (Frederick Copleston, 1962)

2.1: Meta-ethics

Meta-ethics is the term used to describe the study of the meaning of ethical language rather than normative ethics, such as naturalism, which looks at the rightness and wrongness of things.

- Normative ethical theories debated ways of deciding what was 'good', 'bad', 'right' and 'wrong', believing them to have an absolute value, sometimes linking them to religious beliefs.

Naturalism – F.H. Bradley (1846–1924)
Ethical Studies (1876)

- F.H. Bradley's naturalism thought ethical words like 'good', 'bad', 'right' and 'wrong' could be defined in the same way we define 'maths' or 'science', through observation of the natural world.

- What you should or should not do was determined by your status or position in society, and by observing that position, you could clearly see what you ought to do. Your duty was to know yourself and then do your duty.

- Morality could be defined in factual terms and had an absolute nature.

Intuitionism – G.E. Moore (1873–1958)
Principia Ethica (1903)

- Moore thought naturalists had made a mistake in thinking we can observe morals in the way we observe the physical aspects of the universe. You cannot *see* 'wrongness' in the way you can see bread rising.

- Morals are absolute but moral judgements are based on an infallible, intuitive knowledge of good things beyond our regular senses. Good itself cannot be defined in the way naturalists wanted to define it.

Emotivism – A.J. Ayer (1910–89)
Language, Truth and Logic (1936)

- Ayer believed true information is that which can be verified using the scientific method. Facts are either observable or

For the exam you need to know about:

- The use of ethical language.

- The ways in which different scholars have understood how terms such as 'good', 'bad', 'right' and 'wrong' are used when moral statements are made.

logically necessary: moral statements are neither. They are not facts and not meaningful as you cannot scientifically or logically prove them. They are emotive expressions.

- Stevenson developed this idea, saying moral statements express subjective beliefs.

Prescriptivism – R.M. Hare (1919–2002)
The Language of Morals (1952)

- For Hare, moral judgements are prescriptive as they express a view from which certain behaviour is expected or hoped for. When we make a judgement about a colour, such as red, we apply it to all similar red things. Moral judgements have this universal quality, too.

- The only coherent way to behave is to act on judgements that you are prepared to universalise or always follow.

Considering intuitionism, emotivism and prescriptivism

First:

- It is reasonable to challenge the idea that we can scientifically prove moral rightness or wrongness.

- You cannot test for good/bad in the way you test for acid/alkaline.

- Moral codes seem to be linked to cultural and religious ideas, which come from ideas that differ from scientific facts.

However:

- People have a sense of what is good and bad and often a common sense about certain actions, such as murder or rape.

- Perhaps we gain this sense intuitively as Moore argues.

- Intuition cannot be measured or tested, and people clearly seem to have different levels of intuition as they disagree about moral behaviour.

Nevertheless:

- People do expect moral statements to be linked to action and treat them as more than just a feeling.

- People have principles, which inform their moral opinions, and these principles mean they apply their moral codes in a

Names and works

A.J. Ayer, *Language, Truth and Logic* (1936)

F.H. Bradley, *Ethical Studies* (1876)

R.M. Hare, *The Language of Morals* (1952)

G.E. Moore, *Principia Ethica* (1903)

Glossary

Emotivism The idea that all moral statements are expressions of feeling and are meaningless.

Intuition A special sense for detecting morality.

Meta-ethics Theories that debate the meaning of the words 'right', 'wrong', and so on.

Naturalism Moral facts can be deduced through science and logic from the world around us.

Normative ethics Debates what is right, wrong, good or bad, and the systems for determining these.

Prescriptivism The idea that moral statements instruct behaviour or hope to lead to behaviour.

Universalisability The idea that morals have a universal character. It applies in all like situations.

similar way when similar situations appear, so perhaps Hare is right.

In conclusion:

• While there is no scientific evidence for morals, there are other dimensions to human life, such as love, friendship and hope, which cannot be tested in the same way, yet are still meaningful.

• Is Hare's argument that morality has a rational basis more convincing than Moore's, who is unable to account for differences of intuition or prove the intuition process?

Tips for AS exam questions (Foundation Paper)

(a) Explain how meta-ethics is different from normative ethics.

• You could emphasise that normative ethics express moral truths while meta-ethics concerns itself with the meaning of ethical language, adding examples of both types of ethics.

• You could contrast the idea of normative ethics, that there are ways of approaching finding what the right or wrong thing is, with emotivism's idea that no moral statement can have any objective meaning.

• You could discuss how meta-ethics explores in what sense something can be known to be true while normative ethics expresses what is claimed to be true.

(b) 'Everyone knows what "good" means.' Discuss.

• You might like to explore different understandings of the word 'good', including moral and non-moral, objective and subjective.

• You could give examples of differences that people have in describing something as good or bad, contrasting that with the common understanding that many people have when words like 'good' are used.

Critical comments

Moore argued that things that are intrinsically good cannot be defined or analysed: 'If I am asked, "What is good?" my answer is that good is good, and that is the end of the matter. Or if I am asked, "How is good to be defined?" my answer is that it cannot be defined, and that is all I have to say about it.' (G.E. Moore, *Principia Ethica*, 1903)

Ayer's case is that moral statements are emotive and nothing else: 'The presence of an ethical symbol in a proposition adds nothing to its factual content. Thus, if I say to someone, "You acted wrongly in stealing that money," I am not stating anything more than if I had simply said, "You stole that money." In adding that this action is wrong, I am not making any further statement about it. I am simply evincing my moral disapproval of it. It is as if I had said, "You stole that money," in a peculiar tone of horror or written it with the addition of some special exclamation marks.' (A.J. Ayer, *Language, Truth and Logic*, 1936)

2.2: Introduction to moral relativism, Virtue Ethics and Natural Law

For the exam you need to know about:

- Moral relativism, for example, Fletcher's Situation Ethics.
- Virtue Ethics.
- Natural Law.

Moral relativism: Situationism – J. Fletcher (1905–91)
Situation Ethics (1966)

This book looks at Situationism as an example of moral relativism: you may have studied another example, Social Contract, for example. Check your notes and revise what you studied in class.

- Moral relativism holds that moral truth varies depending on culture, time, place and religion, and opposes absolutism, which maintains truths are universal.

- Morals are subjective – subject to the culture, religion, time and place.

- Joseph Fletcher argues that the right choice is that which produces the most loving consequence in the particular situation.

- The morality of actions are relative to the situation and are not dictated by fixed laws with absolute moral norms (rules).

- Fletcher argues that agape (unconditional love) is the only intrinsically good thing and all actions are relative to it.

- The most loving consequence is the end to which an action must aim, so the good act varies according to the situation.

- Situation Ethics points to the examples of Jesus breaking traditional laws to do good in a particular situation. It puts people and their plight over and above laws.

Virtue Ethics – Aristotle
Nicomachean Ethics (4th century BCE)

- Virtue theory asks how a person may become better and defines qualities that make them good. It is focused on qualities of character, not actions, as actions indicate their virtues and vices.

- Aristotle argues that we must practise virtuous behaviour if we are to reach the ultimate end, eudaimonia, or ultimate happiness.

- The virtues are courage, temperance, liberality, munificence, high-mindedness, right ambition, good temper, civility, sincerity, wittiness, modesty and just resentment. We may be excessive or deficient in the virtues and so one must find a 'Golden Mean' between these extremes.

- Virtues offer a way to estimate the substance of character and suggest a route for improvement. By knowing and understanding ourselves we can become better. It has become a popular secular ethical system.

- Alasdair MacIntyre (*After Virtue*, 1981) believes our society has lost track of the virtues. He says that a moral society would be one in which people recognise and accept common virtues.

Natural Law – Thomas Aquinas (c. 1225–74)
Summa Theologica (1273)

- Aristotle said, 'The natural is that which everywhere is equally valid.' Aquinas developed an absolutist and deontological ethical theory, Natural Law, which stated that acts are intrinsically right or wrong.

- Natural Law directs people to their divine destiny. It is the divine law, God's law, as opposed to human law.

- In summary, the law is: 'good is to be done and evil avoided.'

- The law is in scripture (revelation) but can also be deduced through reason, so all may realise it, not just those who have scripture.

- Ignoring reason is ignoring God's command.

- A human being must behave in a way whereby his or her actions are in accordance with the divine purpose for humanity, which is deduced through reason. Aquinas deduced five primary precepts for the purposes of human beings: preserve life, reproduce, educate children, live in society, worship God.

- Good acts are those that must be in accordance with the primary precepts. These good acts are called secondary precepts.

- Acts are intrinsically good or bad. When good acts are done, God's purpose is glorified.

- Human beings may be led by apparent 'goods' that tempt them away from Natural Law.

- Both the intention and the act are important. Both must be done out of charity for others. So, for example, my intention is bad when I give to charity to impress someone, though my exterior action is good.

Considering Situation Ethics

- Situation Ethics is flexible as it takes the complexity of human life into account rather than applying blunt rules that could cause harm.

- It is a subjective ethical system as decisions are made from the point of view of the person in the situation and therefore subject to mistakes or selfishness. It is not always easy to know what the most loving thing to do is.

- The pursuit of a loving end may justify an act many would consider wrong. Sometimes you would need to know the future to know what was right.

Considering Virtue Ethics

- Rather than focusing on actions or consequences, Virtue Ethics encompasses all aspects of life and deals with the question of what it means to be human.

- Virtue Ethics is person-centred rather than act- or end-centred, making it more holistic.

- Virtue Ethics depends on moral duty and moral absolutes, a duty to act virtuously and absolute measures of what is virtuous.

- Virtues are traditional concepts. MacIntyre might argue that we have forgotten the old truths, but then old truths are not necessarily good truths.

- It is not clear how we decide and agree upon what the virtues are or what we do when virtues conflict. For example, in a dangerous war situation, should we be brave or should we be pragmatic? Both are virtues.

Considering Natural Law

- Natural Law lets communities with clear common rules structure and organise moral life. It gives clear unambiguous answers to moral questions in times of moral uncertainty.

- Many cultures have recognised that preserving life, educating, building a good society, and so on, are of central importance, independently of Aquinas.

- However, the idea that there is a single or fixed human nature is simplistic and seems to fly in the face of increasing diversity and the changeable nature of personal identity (such as homosexuality, transexuality, and so on). What is meant by 'natural' today?

Names and works

Thomas Aquinas, *Summa Theologica* (1273)

Aristotle, *Nicomachean Ethics* (4th century BCE)

Joseph Fletcher, *Situation Ethics* (1966)

Alasdair MacIntyre, *After Virtue* (1981)

Glossary

Absolutist An ethical theory that has objective morals which are fixed.

Deontological An ethical theory focused on actions instead of ends.

Natural Law A divine and universal moral law knowable through reason and revelation.

Objective moral norms Moral rules that are fixed/universal.

Moral relativism The view that there are no fixed moral rules.

Situationism The view that acts are good or bad depending on the consequences of the particular situation.

Subjectivism The view that morals are subject to the individual, culture, time, and so on.

Virtues Characteristics of a good person, which must be cultivated and practised.

- It is possible to conclude that there may be precepts, but so far they have not been adequately expressed.

- Natural Law cannot take into account the situation or the consequences of actions.

Tips for AS exam questions (Foundation Paper)

(a) What is meant by moral relativism?

- You might explore how the word 'relative' suggests a truth that is not fixed but can change.

- You could suggest different ways in which it could change, such as over time, according to the situation between cultures/religions, or even individuals.

- You could use Situationism as an example of moral relativism, how it holds that the right thing to do is that which produces the most loving outcome, not that which keeps to a set of rules. This means the right thing can change from one situation to the next.

- A good approach would then be to contrast it with absolutism, which holds there are fixed certain truths for all while relativism implies no objective truth, just the truth for the time, the place or the person. Humans are the measure of truth, not any rational force.

(b) 'The problem with Situation Ethics is that it does not provide any definite answers.' Discuss.

- This is a problem and a strength. Arguably, with no definitive answers there can be no clear advice to help people dealing in difficult situations, where they are personally involved yet left to make their own decision on their own judgement, and it may never be clear that they did the right thing.

- You might like to explore the idea that it would start people on a slippery slope where any act could be justified and that people feel strongly that certain horrendous acts are wrong in all situations, such as genocide or rape.

- On the other hand, you could argue that giving people rules is over-simplistic and restrictive and can actually cause more harm than good in particular circumstances. While people always want clear easy answers, reality is often complex and uncertain and a moral system which can accommodate that environment with integrity could be more helpful than one that denies life's ambiguities.

Critical comments

Pope Pius XII called Situation Ethics an 'individualistic and subjective appeal to the concrete circumstances of actions to justify decisions in opposition to the natural law or God's revealed will.'

The modern philosopher Julia Annas, in assessing Virtue Ethics, notes there is a danger of: 'romantic nostalgia: the feeling that it would be nicer if we could shed the problem-era that we have and go back to a very different set of problems; that ethics would be a kinder, gentler place if we could forget about hard cases and talk about friendship and the good life instead. Like much nostalgia, this is misplaced.' (Julia Annas, in *Philosophical Perspectives 6*, 1992)

3.1: The ontological argument

For the exam you need to know about:

• The ontological argument from Anselm and Descartes.

• The challenges to the ontological argument from Gaunilo and Kant.

The ontological argument for the existence of God – St Anselm (1033–1109)
Proslogion, Chapters 2, 3

• Anselm's argument is a *reductio ad absurdum* argument – an argument that makes a proof by showing that the opposite cannot possibly be true. The ontological argument is an *a priori* argument starting from a definition of God, not experience. The argument is that by understanding the definition, God is proved to exist.

• Anselm says God is 'that than which nothing greater can be conceived'. Something that exists in reality is greater than something that exists only in the mind.

• God must exist because something *can* be thought to be greater than something existing only in the intellect, namely that God exists in reality. God has necessary existence and it is illogical to consider otherwise. There is no possibility of God not existing.

Gaunilo's challenge (and Anselm's reply)
On Behalf of the Fool (11th century)

• A monk called Gaunilo argued against Anselm: we can imagine an island greater than which another cannot be conceived. If it is perfect, perfection includes existence so it must exist. Gaunilo argues this shows the flaw in Anselm's argument: we cannot define things into existence.

• Anselm replied that God is a special case because there can only be one being greater than which another cannot be conceived. There may be a thing greater than a perfect island, but not God. Only God has all the perfections and so the argument can only apply to God.

René Descartes (1596–1650)
Meditations on First Philosophy (1641)

• Descartes also argued that existence cannot be separated from God. He says God is defined as a supremely perfect being and so must exist.

- Existence, singularity and perfection are God's characteristics. In fact, God's essence is existence. If something is supremely perfect, and if existence is a perfection, God, by definition, exists.

- It is a contradiction to think of God not existing in the same way as it is a contradiction to think of a mountain existing without a valley.

Objections to the ontological theory – Immanuel Kant (1724–1804)

- Kant argues that we can only know the world through our experience of it, and we cannot know any aspects of existence beyond our experience. Existence is not a predicate (an attribute or quality) of perfection that a thing can lack. Existence is the thing and all its attributes.

- Kant also argues that Anselm was wrong to suppose that a merely possible necessary being was a contradictory idea. To think of a being as merely possible, one must think away its existence. One is not suppressing existence and leaving other attributes such as omnipotence, one is suppressing the whole thing.

- Existence does not belong to the idea of another being. The fact that we cannot see a contradiction in the idea of God is not evidence that God exists.

Modern versions

- Norman Malcolm (1911–90) (*Anselm's Ontological Argument*, 1960) argues that if God does not exist, then God cannot come into existence, as that would require another force, which would mean God was limited, not God as we define God. If God does exist, God cannot have come into existence nor cease.

- God's existence is either impossible or necessary. It can only be impossible if the idea of God is logically absurd. Assuming that it is not, then God necessarily exists.

- Alvin Plantinga (1932–) (*God, Freedom and Evil*, 1974) develops the idea of infinite possible worlds. In a possible world, a maximally great being could exist (omnipotent, omniscient, morally perfect). For there to be a maximally great being, he would have to exist in all possible worlds, so a maximally great being exists. However, this argument only proves possibility, not actuality.

Evaluating the discussion

- The ontological argument does not rely on proving God's existence empirically, which could be an advantage as different people give subjective interpretations of empirical evidence.

- However, is existence a predicate/attribute of perfection? Arguably not, Kant suggests. To say, 'The cat is black,' adds information about the cat, whereas to say, 'The cat exists,' tells us nothing more about the cat. If 'The cat exists' adds a property, then 'The cat does not exist' takes away a property, and yet it is not a property that is taken away but the cat itself.

- Also, existence means different things in different contexts. Prime numbers exist but they do not have a distinct physical reality.

- As the philosopher Bertrand Russell argues, Anselm's use of the word 'exists' is problematic. If existence is a predicate, the following would be valid: men exist, Father Christmas is a man, therefore Father Christmas exists. Existence is a property for the idea of a thing, not the thing itself.

- Many commentators have noted that it is much easier to be persuaded that ontological arguments are weak than to say exactly what is wrong with them. There is ongoing discussion about their merits.

Tips for AS exam questions

(a) Explain the ontological argument from Anselm and Gaunilo's objections to it.

- Explain the definition of God that Anselm gives and how a thing in reality is greater than in the mind. Explain how this leads Anselm to the conclusion that God exists and that God's existence is logically necessary.

- You could explain that the argument is a *reductio ad absurdum* argument and is *a priori*, starting from a definition of God, not experience.

- Explain Gaunilo's example of an island to show how we cannot define things into existence.

(b) 'The ontological argument can never overcome Kant's objection that existence is not a predicate.' Discuss.

- One approach would be to consider the argument's advantage of non-reliance on empirical evidence and contrast it with Kant's argument that we only know the world through our experience of it.

Names and works

St Anselm, *Proslogion*, Chapters 2, 3

René Descartes, *Meditations on First Philosophy* (1641)

Gaunilo, *On Behalf of the Fool* (11th century)

Immanuel Kant, *Critique of Pure Reason* (1781)

Glossary

A priori At first sight; an argument that does not need sensory experience evidence.

Ontological The metaphysical study of the nature of being and existence.

Predicate An attribute or characteristic of a thing.

- Look at Kant's criticism that existence is not a predicate (attribute or quality) of perfection that a thing can lack.

- Consider whether it is reasonable to move from a definition to something existing and whether that is what Anselm does.

- One possible conclusion could be based around the comment of many philosophers that the ontological argument looks unsound, but it is very difficult to say exactly where it *is* unsound.

Critical comments

'For if I hear about some man completely unknown to me, whom I do not even know exists, I could at least think about him through that specific and generic knowledge by which I know what a man is or what men are like…But when I hear someone say "God" or "something greater than everything else", I cannot think of it as I thought of that non-existent man, for I was able to think of the latter in terms of some truly existing thing known to me, while in the former case I can think only of the bare words, and on this basis alone one can seldom or never gain any true knowledge.' (Gaunilo)

'I try to conceive a being, as the highest reality without any defect, the question still remains, whether it exists or not…the knowledge of that object should be possible *a posteriori* also…and any existence outside that field, the realm of sensory experience, though it cannot be declared to be absolutely impossible, is a presupposition that cannot be justified by anything.' (Kant)

3.2: The cosmological argument

For the exam you need to know about:

- The cosmological argument from Aquinas and Copleston.

- The challenges to the cosmological argument from Hume and Russell.

Introduction

- The cosmological argument is also known as the first cause argument and it contrasts with the ontological argument as it is *a posteriori*, based on sensory experience.

- In this argument, things do not have to exist (there could have been nothing) but things do exist because something has brought them into existence. There is a chain of causes and effects that go back to the beginning of the universe. There must have been a first cause that has necessary existence (does not have a cause otherwise it would not be the first cause) and that first cause must be God.

- Some philosophers, such as Aristotle, call the first cause the Unmoved Mover, or Prime Mover.

The cosmological argument – Thomas Aquinas
Summa Theologica (1273)

- Aquinas developed his 'Five Ways' to prove the existence of God, the first of which was based on motion.

- The world is in motion; there is change, which comes about because of a cause. The changes and causes cannot go back to infinity. There must have been a Prime Mover, an Unmoved Mover, which has no cause and initiated the universe. That Prime Mover is God.

- Things achieve their potential through external influences. For example, fire burns enabling wood to realise its potential of becoming hot. The wood needs the fire to become hot; it cannot become hot on its own otherwise it would already be hot.

- Aquinas' second way is that nothing can cause itself as it would have to exist before it existed to cause itself. Aquinas rejects the idea of an infinite sequence of causes and concludes there must be an uncaused cause, which is God.

- The third way is based on matter in the universe. Things come to exist and cease. There must have been a time when nothing existed, so the cause must be external to it and have always existed, a necessary being, which is God. Without such a cause, nothing would exist.

Copleston's cosmological argument – Frederick Copleston (1907–94)

- This argument was put forward in a radio debate (with Bertrand Russell) in 1948.

- Copleston argued that there are some things in the world that do not have in themselves the reason or cause for their existence.

- The world is the real or imagined totality of individual objects, none of which have within themselves the reason or cause for their existence – they depend upon other causes.

- The universe's explanation must be external to it for the explanation to be complete and it must be a self-explanatory, necessary existent being – God.

Hume's objections – David Hume (1711–76)
Dialogues Concerning Natural Religion (1779)

- Hume argues that it is incorrect to move from stating that everything in the universe has a cause to the universe itself has a cause.

- Hume challenges the idea that the universe has a beginning. Why can it not go back to infinity?

- Hume also argues that even if we accept that the universe must have a cause, there is no solid ground for assuming that this cause must be the Christian God. It could have been caused by a committee of divine beings, for example.

Russell's objections – Bertrand Russell (1872–1970)

- Russell rejects Copleston's terms that everything is either contingent or dependent.

- He argues the universe simply is and there is no need to ask for an explanation – after all, Christians do not feel a need to make God self-explanatory.

- Russell agreed with Hume's criticism. Simply to say that every human has a mother does not imply that the human race has a mother.

Extracts from the 1948 BBC Radio debate on the existence of God

- Copleston:...I can't see how you can rule out the legitimacy of asking the question how the total, or anything at all, comes to be there. Why something rather than nothing, that is the question? The fact that we gain our knowledge of causality empirically, from particular causes, does not rule out the possibility of asking what the cause of the series is...

- Russell: I can illustrate what seems to me your fallacy. Every man who exists has a mother, and it seems to me your argument is that therefore the human race must have a mother, but obviously the human race hasn't a mother – that's a different logical sphere.

- Copleston: Well, I can't really see any parity. If I were saying 'every object has a phenomenal cause, therefore the whole series has a phenomenal cause,' there would be a parity, but I'm not saying that; I'm saying, every object has a phenomenal cause if you insist on the infinity of the series – but the series of phenomenal causes is an insufficient explanation of the series. Therefore the series has not a phenomenal cause but a transcendent cause.

- Russell: That's always assuming that not only every particular thing in the world, but the world as a whole must have a cause. For that assumption I see no ground whatever. If you give me a ground, I'll listen to it.

- Copleston: Well, the series of events is either caused or it's not caused. If it is caused, there must obviously be a cause outside the series. If it's not caused, then it's sufficient to itself, and if it's sufficient to itself, it is what I call necessary. But it can't be necessary since each member is contingent, and we've agreed that the total has no reality apart from its members, therefore it can't be necessary. Therefore it can't be uncaused, therefore it must have a cause...

Names and works

Thomas Aquinas, *Summa Theologica* (1273)

David Hume, *Dialogues Concerning Natural Religion* (1779)

Glossary

Actuality and potentiality Anything changing is changed by something else. Wood will potentially become hot when it burns. When it is burning, it is no longer potentially hot – when actually hot, it is no longer potentially hot. A cause is required.

Sufficient reason Every fact must have an explanation for why it is true.

Tips for AS exam questions

(a) Explain the cosmological argument for the existence of God.

- The argument is a first cause argument; sensory experience tells us that there is a chain of causes and effects, which effect change on things. An uncaused first cause is required, which is God.

- You could explore Aquinas' argument that the world is in motion, change requires a cause, and the idea that infinite recession is less plausible than a Prime Mover.

- You could then describe Aquinas' elimination of the idea that nothing can cause something, the cycle that things appear and cease, and his argument that God is needed to get from nothing to something.

- You could also refer to Copleston's arguments.

(b) 'The cosmological argument is unconvincing.' Discuss.

- Explore the argument that it is unsatisfactory to imagine a world as existing in a succession of different states infinitely and so a first cause necessarily exists. You could refer to Copleston here.

- You could examine the question of why we cannot ask why God exists if we can explain the created universe.

- Does a first cause necessarily have to be the God of Christianity? Would such a God be knowable?

- Can we use knowledge based on experience to make conclusions about things beyond experience?

Critical comments

'The success of the cosmological argument depends first of all on a willingness to ask the question, "Why is there a universe?" If you are content to simply accept that the universe is there and does not need an explanation, or that it can be explained by infinite regress, then the cosmological argument fails. In addition, God must also be shown to be a simpler or better ultimate explanation than the brute fact of the existence of the universe, and the idea of an uncaused cause which transcends the distinction between something and nothing must be shown to be credible.' (Peter Vardy, *The Puzzle of God*, 1990)

3.3: The teleological argument

For the exam you need to know about:

- The teleological argument from Aquinas and Paley.
- The challenges to the teleological argument from Hume, Mill and Darwinism.

The teleological (design) argument

- 'Telos' means 'end'. The teleological or design argument is *a posteriori* because it relies on evidence from sensory experience of the natural order of the world – the evidence points to a designer.

- 'What could be more clear or obvious when we look up to the sky and contemplate the heavens, than that there is some divinity of superior intelligence.' (Cicero (106–43 BCE), *De Natura Deorum*)

- The argument is that the universe has, on the one hand, a clear order and regularity, and on the other hand, purpose. It is of sufficient complexity to suggest the work of a designer who is God.

- The order and regularity of the universe has been compared to a well-kept garden that could not have happened by chance.

- The designer's work, the universe, is constructed to fulfil a specific divine purpose.

- Evidence can be found in the sophistication of the human eye, the order of seasons, and the solar system, for example.

Aquinas' teleological argument
Summa Theologica and *Summa contra Gentiles* (1273)

- The fifth of Aquinas' Five Ways shows that natural bodies act in regularity to fulfil certain ends.

- In this, inorganic objects cannot direct themselves. The world works in harmony for a single aim, indicating an intelligent designer; for example, in the way an arrow is directed by an archer.

The teleological argument – William Paley (1743–1805)
Natural Theology (1802)

- If one found a watch lying on the ground, one would think it was designed even if one did not know the purpose of it or the designer.

- The intricacy of the mechanisms of a human resembles a

watch with a definite purpose and so can only be explained by the presence of an intelligent and purposive agency.

- Paley argues that the evidence from astronomy and Newton's laws of gravity indicates a regularity that must have been imposed by an external designer.

The Anthropic Principle – F.R. Tennant (1866–1957)
Philosophical Theology (1930)

- The universe seems to have been designed for intelligent life. Had the Big Bang been any bigger or smaller, the planets could not have formed – it had precisely the required force. The timing was perfect for the development of life. There is a chain of coincidences that makes life possible. It suggests intention and purpose, implying God.

- The world can be analysed in a rational manner. It has all the material necessary for life and evolution allows for the development of an intelligent human life, part of God's plan. A chaotic universe could have been possible, which would not have led to humanity.

- Tennant also makes an aesthetic argument that humans can appreciate their surroundings, art, music and literature, which is not necessary for survival or natural selection and implies a creator.

Hume's challenges
Dialogues Concerning Natural Religion (1779)

- The teleological argument states that the complexity of the world implies a designer but the designer's mind is also complex. Hume asked, why stop at God when asking for explanations?

- The presence of evil in the world suggests the designer God is either not entirely good or not powerful enough, rather than the God of classical theism. Perhaps the world was completed by an inferior being rather than such a being as God.

- Why should there only be one designer? Many could have participated in the design.

- The design argument simplistically portrays God as a super-human who makes things just as people make things.

Names and works

Thomas Aquinas, *Summa Theologica* and *Summa contra Gentiles* (1273)

Charles Darwin, *The Origin of Species* (1859)

David Hume, *Dialogues Concerning Natural Religion* (1779)

John Stuart Mill, *Three Essays on Religion* (1850–8)

William Paley, *Natural Theology* (1802)

Glossary

Anthropic Pinciple The theory that the universe depends upon a series of coincidences, implying a creator.

Telos Greek word meaning 'end'.

- A machine is not a good analogy for the universe. Perhaps a better one would be a growing thing – something that develops on its own.

- There is no evidence of the universe being made. We should not argue from causes within the universe to the cause of the universe.

Challenges from John Stuart Mill (1806–73)
Three Essays on Religion (1850–8)

- While the teleological argument might point to a God, it would not point to a Christian God who was all-good and all-powerful because of the damage done by natural disasters.

- The suffering caused by natural disasters is the kind of suffering humans are punished for when they are the cause. If the maker is all-powerful, then we must conclude the maker wills suffering.

The Darwinian challenge

- Charles Darwin (1809–82) (*The Origin of Species*, 1859) proposed the theory of natural selection whereby new species could evolve from existing ones without the need for an intervention from an external being.

- The complex intricacies in nature are explained by this process of evolution as only the fittest survive. A designer God is not necessary and the so-called designed universe is in fact a naturally evolved one.

- In the Bible, Genesis suggested that God created the universe including the living creatures, such as human beings, while natural suggestions implies animals, including humans, evolved.

- From the Christian perspective, Genesis says humans fell from grace to sin, while Darwin envisaged humans rising into rationality.

Tips for AS exam questions

(a) Explain Paley's teleological argument.

- You could start by explaining what is meant by 'teleological'. Use the example of the watch as an indicator that a designer exists to illustrate the argument about the universe as clearly designed.

- Explore the idea of the universe having purposive agency,

made with a purpose, in the same way as a watch has. You could refer to astronomy and Newtonian physics as illustrative of this.

(b) 'Paley's teleological argument cannot meet the challenges of Darwinism.' Discuss.

- Explain what natural selection is and the extent to which it replaces the need of a designer to explain purposive agency.

- You could explain the case that the universe's complexity does not need a designer but exists because it is the only universe that can exist.

- You could consider the opposing view that Darwinism cannot explain why there is a universe as opposed to nothing.

- You could consider whether Paley's teleological argument can incorporate natural selection as a feature of the design.

Critical comments

'…if every time we turned a rock over we saw the message "Made by God" stamped on it, then I guess everybody would have to assume that we did live in a universe of His design. It has to be a matter of personal taste whether you regard the accumulated evidence as compelling enough to want to make that leap. But, inevitably, it is outside the scope of science as such. Science deals with the facts of the world, religion deals with the interpretation of those facts.' (Paul Davies, in *Science and Wonders*, 1996)

3.4: The moral argument

For the exam you need to know about:

• The moral argument from Kant, and challenges to it from Freud.

Kant's moral argument
Groundwork of the Metaphysic of Morals (1785);
Critique of Practical Reason (1788); *The Metaphysics of Morals* (1797)

• Moral people must act out of duty rather than a personal desired end to pursue the highest good. If people feel obliged to act out of duty, they must have freedom to act. 'Ought implies can.' A moral action must be one that is possible to do.

• Happiness is an end everyone seeks and Kant argued that a world where all people were moral and happy was the highest good (*summum bonum*), which people are obliged to bring about. In a perfect world, moral behaviour should lead to happiness. Some moral choices may be good but nevertheless cause unhappiness, especially if personal sacrifice is necessary.

• God must exist to ensure that all can achieve that which they are morally required to pursue – the greatest happiness. Not all virtuous acts would lead to happiness hence the necessity for the possibility of a Heaven with God in which all may be good and happy.

• It is illogical to be required to seek an impossible end. God's existence is morally necessary. If we are to live as a moral being, we must believe that we live and act in a moral world, even if it does not appear as such.

• Kant rejects theoretical arguments to prove God's existence. A rational, moral person should believe in God. We do not need God to be able to recognise what is morally right, but morality does lead to belief in God: 'The moral law leads to religion.' (Kant)

Other versions of the moral argument

• Cardinal Newman (1801–90) (*Grammar of Assent*, 1870) argues that God's existence is deduced from the presence of conscience. Our sense of guilt, moral obligation and responsibility is a sense of God.

• Robert Adams (*The Virtue of Faith and Other Essays in Philosophical Theology*, 1987) argues that wrongness can be identical to being contrary to the commands of a

▶

loving God. If God does not exist, or God is not loving, then nothing can be morally right or wrong. If some things are wrong, then God must exist.

Names and works

Sigmund Freud, *The Outline of Psychoanalysis* (1938)

Immanuel Kant, *Groundwork of the Metaphysic of Morals* (1785); *Critique of Practical Reason* (1788); *The Metaphysics of Morals* (1797)

Challenges to the moral argument – Sigmund Freud (1856–1939)
The Outline of Psychoanalysis (1938)

- Arguably, the objective duty that Kant believes in has come from social conditioning and human nature, not from God. Freud saw conscience as guilt. Children learn that the world restricts these desires and they create the ego, which takes account of the realities of the world and society. A 'superego' internalises and reflects the anger and disapproval of others.

- A guilty conscience is created, which grows into a life and power of its own, irrespective of the rational thought and reflection of the individual. The mature and healthy conscience is the ego's reflection on the best way of achieving integrity. The immature conscience (the superego) is a mass of feelings of guilt.

- Conscience is the product of the unconscious mind, or superego, which is a parental policeman that we create within ourselves during our upbringing. It then restrains our actions with the sense of guilt. Our moral awareness has nothing to do with God.

- In Freud's view, morality does not have the objectivity that Kant claimed. He challenges Kant by saying that our experience of a sense of right and wrong does not have to point to a divine moral law-giver, there could be an alternative human explanation for our moral sense, which he provides.

The strengths and weaknesses of the arguments

- The moral argument appeals to our own experience; we have all experienced the sense of injustice if wrongly accused, or of feeling good when we have done something kind, for example, so it is appealing to think that we all share an innate moral sense.

- A weakness might be that there is no logical reason why the cause of our sense of morality might be God. Other people, such as Freud, have offered alternative explanations.

Glossary

Summum bonum The greatest happiness; a world of happy, virtuous people.

Superego Internalised moral authority that imposes senses of guilt, moral responsibility and obligation based on upbringing.

- Richard Swinburne (*The Existence of God*, 1979) rejects the moral argument by arguing that moral principles are analytically and necessarily true. A theistic explanation is not needed.

- However, many dispute that morals are necessarily true (for example, Ayer and Nietzsche).

- Many do not believe in God but do believe in morality, and arguably it could be based on human needs and desires, self-interest and the structure of human nature of society.

- Some challenge the existence of an objective law and that morality could be more to do with personal opinion (such as emotivism). As people disagree over moral issues, this could be evidence that there is no link with God (see also moral relativism, Situation Ethics).

- The moral argument could only ever indicate the existence of the lawmaker. It does not necessarily require the God of classical theism.

- The moral argument may strengthen aspects of beliefs held by people who already believe in God, as those who believe in God link morality to God, but unbelievers may not be persuaded to believe in God on that basis alone.

- Some have argued that people who already accept objective moral laws implicitly believe in a reality of some kind and so have made a step towards God.

Tips for AS exam questions

(a) Explain Kant's moral argument for the existence of God.

- Explain that Kant offers a rational justification for believing in God.

- You could explore the idea of good will and duty, 'ought implies can,' and the greatest good, *summum bonum*, which moral people work towards.

- You could explain that the *summum bonum* must be attainable as a reward for personal sacrifice and pursuit of virtuous behaviour, and yet it is not possible by human effort alone in this world, so there must be an afterlife that requires God to ensure we reach it.

- It is illogical to be required to seek an impossible end. God's existence is morally necessary.

(b) Assess the strengths and weaknesses of the moral argument for the existence of God.

- You might discuss whether the possibility that there are no moral laws removes the necessity for a God or simply undermines the moral argument.

- You could evaluate the case for a morality that does not require God if it is based on human needs and desires, self-interest and the structure of human nature of society.

- You could discuss whether the moral argument requires a lawmaker, not the God of classical theism, and whether it is only likely to encourage believers and discourage atheists.

- You could challenge the assumption that we all share a moral sense – some people do not seem to have one.

Critical comments

'If, as is the case, we feel responsibility, are ashamed, are frightened, at transgressing the voice of conscience, this implies that there is One to whom we are responsible, before whom we are ashamed, whose claims upon us we fear...If the cause of these emotions does not belong to the visible world, the object to which perception is directed must be supernatural and divine.' (John Henry Newman, *Grammar of Assent*, 1870)

'In this manner, the moral laws lead through the conception of the *summum bonum* as the object and final end of pure practical reason to religion, that is, to the recognition of all duties as divine commands, not as sanctions, that is to say, arbitrary ordinances of a foreign and contingent in themselves, but as essential laws of every free will in itself, which, nevertheless, must be regarded as commands of the Supreme Being, because it is only from a morally perfect (holy and good) and at the same time all-powerful will, and consequently only through harmony with this will, that we can hope to attain the *summum bonum* which the moral law makes it our duty to take as the object of our endeavours.' (Immanuel Kant, *Critique of Practical Reason*, 1788)

3.5: Arguments from religious experience

For the exam you need to know about:

- Arguments for religious experience from William James.

- Challenges to it from Freud and Marx.

Religious experience of God

- Religious experience is an experience of a supernatural nature, possibly by an individual, which might happen spontaneously, such as, in Judaeo-Christian beliefs, Samuel hearing God call him.

- A religious experience draws a person into closer awareness of knowledge of the divine. They may occur in prayer, may be life changing, and may bring a person into union with God.

- Rudolph Otto (1869–1937) (*The Idea of the Holy*, 1936) uses the word 'numinous' to mean being in the presence of an awesome power. Martin Buber (1878–1963) uses 'I–thou' to mean taking a personal relationship deeper. God is the eternal thou into which a person may enter a relationship.

- Religious experience may be mystical, recognising knowledge of the ultimate reality beyond normal understanding, being released from the physical constraints of the world and the self, and a sense of bliss and unity with the divine. Some experiences come through entering states of consciousness through prayer, contemplation, meditation or even dance. In this state, the mystic feels a powerful sense of understanding, union with the other, no longer distracted by the physical world or the yearnings of the self, and sometimes ecstasy.

- Swinburne argues that religious experiences may be public, in which God is seen to be acting in a situation, perhaps breaking laws of nature, or private, such as dreams, mystical events or a sense of being guided by God.

William James (1842–1910)
The Varieties of Religious Experience (1902)

- Religious experiences are ineffable, which means difficult to explain. They are not empirical but private inner events.

St Teresa of Avila could not fully describe the religious experiences she had.

- James classifies and typifies religious experience. They have a noetic quality, which provides a sense of truth not perceived by intellect. They are transient in that they may last between a few moments and a couple of hours, though they have great meaning and can affect the person fundamentally. During the experience, the person is passive – they lose control, being overwhelmed by God.

- Religious experience is evidence for God's existence to the individual. The experience may come through prayer, worship or meditation, creative acts, the sense of community, the love of God as felt through others. They may involve messengers from God such as angels. These experiences cannot be rationally or empirically measured as they are spiritual in nature.

- For James, religious experiences lead to consistency, stability and flowing human relations.

Swinburne's case for religious experience
The Existence of God (1979)

- The Principle of Credulity supports using the experience as evidence of God. The principle means that we should accept what appears to be the case unless there is good evidence against the experience. If the experience seems genuine, then this is evidence for God's existence.

- The Principle of Testimony is that in the absence of evidence against, we should rely on the reports that we hear. It is reasonable to believe people.

- The writer Peter Vardy challenges these principles. For example, some people genuinely believe to have encountered UFOs. Before accepting the accounts, it is reasonable to seek additional information to clarify, such as radar evidence or meteorological reports. These are reasonable precautions to take before accepting an unusual event and could apply to religious experience.

Freud's challenge
The Future of an Illusion (1927)

- Freud sees religion as a collective neurosis that prevents people from falling into individual neuroses and psychoses.

A friend experiences an 'oceanic feeling', a lack of sense of ego, no boundaries between himself and the world at large, which is the source of his belief.

- Freud argues that the 'oceanic feeling' is a form of infantile regression in which the person seeks to return to early childhood experiences of breastfeeding. A baby feeding at the mother's breast is an image of peace and comfort. Freud equates the mystic's religious experience with a desire to return to the infantile bliss. It is sustained by fear of the superior power of fate.

Challenges to the argument – Karl Marx (1818–83)
Critique of Hegel's Dialectic and General Philosophy (1844)

- Religion gives false meaning to the empty lives of the downtrodden. It is the 'opiate of the people'.

- Spiritual alienation arises from socio-economic deprivation. Religious activity masks economic inequality, giving false illusions of fulfilment. Religious experiences are generated by oppressive social conditions.

- Religion divides the world into a heavenly and an earthly realm. There is heavenly justification for earthly injustice and heavenly consolation for earthly misery.

Evaluating the discussion

- One might assess whether the experience corresponds to something in the real world, but one relies on the subjective account of the experience, not empirical evidence.

- One might try to assess the experience by looking for internal inconsistencies to disprove a divine source, but this uses intellectual criteria to assess something that is difficult to put into words by the perceiver.

- One might try to assess the experience by focusing on the consequences, whether they are life enhancing or diminishing, but this requires assumptions about what should be communicated, which cannot be tested.

- The experience cannot be empirically tested as it is subjective. While someone who has had a religious experience may be convinced themselves, and sound convincing to others, this in itself does not make God's existence necessary.

- Different religious experiences are perceived in different ways, so there is no consistency to validate that experience. It is not necessary that such experiences should be alike.

- For a believer, a religious experience is evidence of God's existence and may strengthen their faith, though it can simply raise the possibility that God exists to a non-believer.

- Experience is deceptive. Drugs may induce experiences, hallucinations may occur, or genuine mistakes can be made in interpreting what one perceives. Psychological mindset may affect the ability to evaluate an experience. However, not all experiences fall into these categories. Religious experience is not necessarily one of these and if it is, what is to say that God cannot use natural causes?

- Some reject religious experience, believing God is an impossible idea. This fails to consider the actual experience but simply interprets it in the light of a belief.

Tips for AS exam questions

(a) Explain how followers of Marx have challenged the idea that religious experience is evidence for the existence of God.

- Marx argued that religious experiences are generated by oppressive social conditions.

- You could describe and explain Marx's account of religion as the 'opiate of the people'.

- You could explore the link between lack of money/status and lack of spirituality. Consider religion's masking activity and wish fulfilment.

- The Marxist view is that heavenly justification and consolation is created to compensate against earthly injustice and misery.

(b) 'Religious experience is the most convincing evidence for God's existence.' Discuss.

- You could refer to William James' work on the evidence of religious experience as being difficult to explain; private inner experiences that are powerful for the individual and not open to external scrutiny.

- You might contrast this with the view that there are other explanations for those experiences such as psychological ones.

- You could discuss whether personal experiences are always going to be more persuasive to the individual who experiences them but not persuasive to the individual that does not.

Names and works

Sigmund Freud, *The Future of an Illusion* (1927)

William James, *The Varieties of Religious Experience* (1902)

Karl Marx, *Critique of Hegel's Dialectic and General Philosophy* (1844)

Critical comments

'It seems that although various objections can be made to the view that it is unreasonable to believe in God on the basis of experience, the whole notion of an experience of God either collapses into something that looks like the notion of being convinced by an argument or is just very difficult to understand. Experience of dogs and cats and people is one thing, but experience of what God is supposed to be seems quite elucidated, let alone judged as something to which one could appeal as providing a reasonable ground for belief in God. This conclusion is independent of any reason apart from experience which we may have for believing in God, and, of course, there are evidently people who would disagree with it.' (Brian Davies, *An Introduction to the Philosophy of Religion*, 1993)

3.6: The problem of evil

For the exam you need to know about:

- The problem of evil.
- The classic theodicies of Augustine and Irenaeus.

The problem of evil

- The God of classical theism is held to be omnipotent, omniscient and the wholly good creator of the world, so why is evil present? Augustine said, 'Either God cannot abolish evil, or He will not; if He cannot, then He is not all-powerful; if He will not, then He is not all-good.' (*Confessions*, c. 400)

- There is great moral evil in that human beings do terrible things to each other. In the twentieth century, there were several acts of genocide, violent and sexual crime is a problem in society, and there are examples where minors are abused and killed by adults.

- There is a considerable amount of suffering caused by natural evil. Hurricanes, tornadoes, earthquakes and volcanic eruptions destroy homes and lives. There are also many diseases and other medical problems that people suffer from such as cancer.

Theodicy of Irenaeus (130–202)

- God wanted a perfect world but that perfection could only come through human free will. Humanity was first created as an immature, imperfect being that had yet to grow and develop. Moral evil is the consequence of this freedom. In Christian teaching, Adam did not 'fall' from grace but erred due to immaturity.

- Humans could freely choose to become good and turn to God. The world is 'soul making' and evil helps the development from imperfection to Godlike. Natural evil, such as famine, was God's way of creating a place that develops people's personal qualities, for example, encouraging compassion.

- Evil is necessary and will make people better. When people die, they either go straight to Heaven or will continue their soul-making journey until they do.

- God is partly responsible for evil as it is a means by which people grow and learn. God made the world imperfect.

Strengths and weaknesses of Irenaeus' theodicy

- Allowing everyone into Heaven seems to excuse evil people

unless the purification of the soul is not an easy process. Eternal damnation can seem unjust. Perhaps the terrible evil and suffering found in the world is justified by eventual, perfect salvation for all.

- Could a good God lovingly use evil to form his created people? Is extreme evil acceptable on the basis that it is soul making?

- Why not create a morally perfect world that did not have evil and suffering? Some philosophers argue that such a world would be morally static. There would be no good or evil.

- Irenaeus says that human perfection could not be given, but he does not justify this claim. Why could God have not just created humans morally perfect?

- Suffering seems to be so unevenly distributed, suggesting God does not want some people to make any spiritual progress because they lead such happy uneventful lives, whereas other people have a terrible time and some turn away from God as a result. We do not see much evidence of people becoming more spiritually aware when they suffer more.

Theodicy of Augustine (354–430)

- God is good and perfect and made a flawless world. True happiness is found in the eternal, that is, God, not in the human self or material objects.

- Humans have free will. They may turn to the eternal God for happiness or to temporal material goods instead. Only God can truly satisfy humans but humans cannot clearly see God.

- Humans are aware of the truth that God provides happiness and are also aware of eternal moral laws in the heart that should guide their free will. Moral perfection is loving God, turning one's heart to God, and doing God's will.

- Turning the will from God to a material good is evil. Goodness is caused by divine goodness. Evil is created by the free will turning away from divine goodness in the way that Adam and Eve turned away from God.

- Evil is 'that which falls away from essence and tends to non-being…It tends to make that which is cease to be.' (*De moribus eccl.*, 2.2.2)

- Everything in God is ordered but there is disorder in the will that turns away. In the privation of good, there is disorder for which the will is responsible.

- Moral evil is the privation of right order in the human will. The people are divided between those who turn to God and those who turn away. Evil is a privation and not a positive thing, so it is not created by God.

- Natural evil is deserved suffering in response to sin.

Strengths and weaknesses of Augustine's theodicy

- The idea that evil is not a thing but a privation makes sense and the free will defence explains moral evil.

> - F.E.D. Schleiermacher (1768–1834) (*The Christian Faith*, 1821) says it is logically contradictory to argue that a perfect world went wrong and evil emerged, as it suggests it came from nothing. Either it was imperfect from the start or it was allowed to go wrong.

- If the world was created good and humans had no knowledge of good or evil, how could they be free to obey or disobey God?

- The existence of Hell or eternal torment challenges the idea of an all-loving God. If Hell is part of God's design and God knew things would go wrong, why did God allow it to happen? This implies a malicious God.

- Not all who suffer have sinned. A baby who suffers has not sinned and cannot be blamed for original sin.

- It also demands belief in a medieval worldview that people do not all share today.

Modern debates over the problem of evil

- Like Irenaeus, Hick argues that God's main purpose is to bring humans from animal self-centredness to moral and spiritual maturity. Humans are created imperfect and distanced (epistemic distance) from God. If God were too close to humans, their knowledge of God would overcome their freedom. The world and the evil within it are designed to enable humans to mature. In Heaven, all the wrongs are put right.

- Swinburne, like Augustine, sees free will as a central factor. Humans could not have been created free

▶

Names and works

Augustine, *De moribus eccl.*, 2.2.2.

Irenaeus, *Against Heresies* (c. 181)

Glossary

Moral evil Evil caused by human intention and action.

Natural evil Evil caused by natural disasters.

Process theodicy The argument that God is not the all-powerful God of classical theism but is a limited being within the universe who can only encourage good, not ensure it.

Soul making The process of improvement through suffering.

without the capacity to do evil as well as good. Natural evil is necessary so that humans can learn what causes pain and suffering and therefore learn about the effects of evil as well as good.

- Alfred North Whitehead and David Griffin argue for a process theodicy, modifying the conventional understanding of God's omnipotence. God has unlimited persuasive power rather than coercive power. God did not create the universe and cannot break the laws of nature. Evil is beyond God's power to stop and God in fact suffers when it is done.

- Process theodicy answers the main question by denying the omnipotence of God, and the idea of a God who suffers makes God seem sympathetic to the human condition. However, there is no guarantee of triumph in the end, so what is the point of human moral behaviour?

- The existence of evil does not rule out the existence of God, though it may challenge what is meant by the goodness of God or the traditional nature of the God of classical theism.

Tips for AS exam questions

(a) Explain how the theodicy of Irenaeus differs from that of Augustine.

- Place Irenaeus and Augustine in their historical context. Irenaeus comes first.

- You could show how Irenaeus accounted for evil by suggesting that God allows it to continue as part of God's plan for humanity. Evil is necessary for human freedom.

- You could also note that Augustine, however, felt evil does not exist as a separate thing but is in fact a privation of good. It is a necessary part of the created world in that for humans to be free to turn to God they must be free to turn away.

- Suffering in the world results from the fall of angels and human evil. God did not create evil or intend it to exist.

- The main differences lie in the nature of evil and its purpose and origin.

(b) 'Natural evil is not explained by the need for free will.' Discuss.

- You could show your understanding of the distinction between moral and natural evil and the link between human free action and moral evil.

- You could explain why natural evil is more difficult to attribute to human action, but also consider Augustine's link with the fall of Adam and Eve.

- You might explore Irenaeus' approach, suggesting that natural evil is important for our free will to develop and be educated, even if its origins cannot be attributed to humankind.

Critical comments

'Our "solution", then, to this baffling problem of excessive and underserved suffering is a frank appeal to the positive power of mystery. Such suffering remains unjust and inexplicable, haphazard and cruelly excessive...suffering is a real mystery, impenetrable to the rationalising human mind.' (John Hick, *Evil and the God of Love*, 1978)

'Religious belief is ultimately a faith relationship with reality itself...It is to make a life investment, to stake one's life on an "if". There are no guarantees, merely a history accounted for by believers in a certain way and a knowledge in one's own heart that one has an immense capacity for love as well as the enormous potential of an individual human being to stand against the forces of evil and, in the end, to overcome them.' (Peter Vardy, *The Puzzle of Evil*, 1992)

For the exam you need to know about:

- The challenges of psychology and sociology to religious belief in terms of the ways these disciplines approach an understanding of religion.

Psychology and religious belief

Freud and religious belief

Totem and Taboo (1913)

- Freud believed religion was an illusion based on desires. Inner psychological conflict combined with tensions caused by living in society and the fears of the environment produce a need. Religion offers images and ideas, 'wish fulfilment', to help overcome these problems.

- Freud believed religion answered a person's inner needs but was a neurotic illness or behaviour caused by traumatic (often sexual) memories suppressed in the unconscious mind.

- Patients suffering from hysteria caused by suppressed memories show obsessive compulsive behaviour. Religious people are obsessed by ritual behaviour in the same way.

- Sexual development causes trauma because the libido is a powerful influence on the human psyche. The Oedipus complex (a desire in the child to possess the parent of the opposite sex and ambivalence to the parent of the same sex) causes conflict in the child's mind.

- At the time, it was thought that in primitive societies there was a dominant male who was hated and venerated by younger males.

- Religion results from sexual guilt. When people suffer from guilt, they create idols to direct the guilt towards making reparation and seeking forgiveness. The idol is treated like the father, with both hatred and veneration, and eventually the father takes on divine status.

- The desires of the individual conflict with the rules of society, causing tension. Religion provides a reason to submit to the authority of society by promising a reward for the suffering afterwards. It motivates sublimation.

- Death causes fear, which religion relieves by suggesting that natural forces can be controlled through religious devotion.

- Freud's theory does not prove God does not exist. Beliefs derived from deep psychological needs tended to be false; without further evidence to back religion, it must be false.

- Religion has helped people by calming them and giving them hope, but it can also be destructive. Forgiving sinners allows them to sin again.

Religious belief – Carl Gustav Jung (1857–1961)
Psychology and Religion (1960)

- Jung rejected many of Freud's ideas including the claim that religion was a neurosis caused by sexual trauma and was a dangerous entity.

- Jung postulated that the mind was divided into personal unconscious and the older collective unconscious – blueprints of a whole range of primordial ideas, including the concept of God, held in the structure of the mind.

- Jung called the psyche that created these images the archetype. The archetype self creates religious images. People are born with the tendency to generate religious images. Religious experience is caused by an external force and comes from a part of the mind we cannot know about.

- God exists as a psychic reality, but whether God is real cannot be known.

- While Freud thought religion was a neurosis, Jung thought it helped stabilise the mind. The various archetypes needed to be integrated into the personality of the person. This was called 'individuation'. It took place after the person had come to terms with the externals of other people and society around them.

- Individuation was the process of assimilating the unconscious aspect of the person. It is controlled by the archetype the self, which seeks wholeness and generates images of wholeness, which includes religious images. The person achieves wholeness through these images and without them can lead to neurosis.

Sociology and religious belief

Religious belief – Emile Durkheim (1858–1917)
The Elementary Forms of the Religious Life (1912)

- God and society are one. The experience of society gives rise to many ideas including God. God is a symbol created by humans, representing their experience of the power of society.

- God is given power by society and society is empowered by the religious symbolisation. Religion is an instrument of society. It is one of the forces that creates a sense of moral obligation to adhere to society's demands and holds society together.

- 'Society cannot make its influence felt unless it is in action, and it is not in action unless individuals who compose it are assembled together and act in common.'

Names and works

Emile Durkheim, *The Elementary Forms of the Religious Life* (1912)

Sigmund Freud, *Totem and Taboo* (1913)

Carl Gustav Jung, *Psychology and Religion* (1960)

Glossary

Archetype The psyche that creates inner images.

Collective unconscious Blueprints of a whole range of primordial ideas, including the concept of God, held in the structure of the mind.

Idol The substitute object to which guilt about the father and veneration is offered.

Individuation Jung's religious activity that seeks wholeness.

Wish fulfilment Freud's definition for religion; wishes to counter anxieties of life.

- Sacred activities are valued by the community of believers not as means to ends but because the community has bestowed meaning. Religion binds people together.

- Religion is a social creation and is society made divine. God is a projection of the power of society, not a supernatural entity. When sacred things are celebrated, people unwittingly celebrate the power of their society.

- Religion helps humans through the stages of life.

- The disappearance of traditional religion need not lead to the dissolution of society. Modern people can recognise directly that dependence on society which before they recognised through the medium of religious representations.

- Society is the father of all and it is to society that is owed the profound debt of gratitude previously given to God.

Evaluating the debate

- H.H. Farmer (*Towards Belief in God*, 1942) criticises Durkheim's sociological challenge, arguing that religion can lead people beyond normal society to create moral relationships with humans. Religious minds challenge society and go beyond its norms, leading at times to revolution. A prophet can hardly be speaking out against society on behalf of society.

- Much of Freud's evidence has been discredited in psychology today, including the Oedipus complex (for example, some societies are matriarchal), the assumptions about primal communities, and the uses of idols (which in most societies did not happen).

- Freud relied on a particular Judaeo-Christian understanding of religion. Non-conformist Protestant Christianity does not have obsessive ritualistic behaviour, however. Buddhism and Hinduism also create many difficulties in applying his theory.

- Critics of Jung's psychological challenge argue that by stating the psychic is unknowable he protects his theory from disproof.

- An alternative justification for the common images people have is not Jung's archetypes but simply common experiences. The archetype is not necessarily the instinct for God.

- The images projected by archetypes are not the same as religious experiences of God and yet Jung equates the two.

- Atheists are likely to feel justified by the work of Freud and Durkheim, while believers are likely to disregard them and may embrace the work of Jung.

- John Hick argues that both the psychological and sociological arguments against God are not proven. They may be true but they have not demonstrated that they are true.

Tips for AS exam questions

(a) Describe sociological challenges to religious belief.

- You could start by describing how Durkheim's account of religion links it to the expression and instrument of society, not a divine being. Society uses religion to create moral obligation and binds people together.

- Modern people can recognise directly that dependence on society which before they recognised through the medium of religious representations. Religious belief is no longer needed.

- The idea that God is a projection of the power of society, not a supernatural entity, may well reinforce atheists and possibly agnostics, though believers are likely to reject them.

(b) How far can sociological insights aid an understanding of religious belief?

- You could explain how Durkheim's account may be correct in understanding religious structures in social terms and sheds light on the cultural and philosophical influence that might bear on religion.

- You might suggest that religion as a corporate body has to be understood in its social setting.

- However, you could also explore the case that religions often do not accept social norms and sometimes challenge them fundamentally, that some religions are social transformers, not social enforcers, giving examples.

- You might argue that sociological insights tend to generalise the personal dimension of religious belief, such as the particular religious experiences that people have, which may inform their belief.

Critical comments

'The responsible sceptic, whether agnostic or atheist, is not concerned with denying that religious people have had certain experiences as a result of which they have become convinced of the reality of God. The sceptic believes, however, that these experiences can be adequately accounted for without postulating a God, by adopting instead a naturalistic interpretation of religion.' (John Hick, *Philosophy of Religion*, 1973)

4.1: Kant and the Categorical Imperative

For the exam you need to know about:

- Kant and the Categorical Imperative.

- The relationship between this ethical theory and religious methods of ethical decision-making.

Immanuel Kant
Groundwork of the Metaphysic of Morals (1785)

- Kant's theory is deontological. It is based on duty. To act morally is to do one's duty and one's duty is to obey the moral law. One should act out of duty, not emotion or feeling.

- The fact that we ought to do something implies we can do it: 'ought implies can', so moral statements are prescriptive and imply that action will follow.

- Humans seek an ultimate end, the *summum bonum*, and smaller ends are pursued to lead to this great end, though it cannot be reached in this life, so our souls are immortal.

The moral law

- 'Two things fill the mind with…awe…the starry heavens above me and the moral law within me.' (Kant, *Critique of Practical Reason*, 1788) The objective moral law is known through reason.

- Statements of knowledge are either *a priori* analytic (knowable without reference to experience and knowable within the internal logic of the sentence; for example, all spinsters are women) or *a posteriori* synthetic (knowable through experience using empirical measurements; for example, the squirrel is behind the tree).

- Moral statements are *a priori* synthetic. We cannot use empirical measurements for testing morality, so our knowledge of it is gained through pure reason, though we may be mistaken and moral statements may be right or wrong.

Good will and duty

- 'Good will shines forth like a precious jewel…It is impossible to conceive anything at all in the world, or even out of it, which can be taken as good without qualification, except a good will.' (Kant, *Groundwork of the Metaphysic of Morals*, 1785) Other things, such as wealth, can be used for good or bad.

- Good will is the highest form of good and is not dependent on consequences: a will that acts for the sake of duty rather than consequence or emotion. The will is supremely autonomous and free. Freedom is necessary for morality to be possible.

- A person who gives the correct change acts in accordance with the good will, but he or she may be simply being prudent – an honest trader will get more business. A good will is one that acts out of duty alone and not prudence or anything else.

- Actions performed for the sake of duty have moral worth. Duty is acting out of reverence for the law, which is objective and universal.

The Imperatives

- A Hypothetical Imperative is a requirement for something if you want to achieve something else: a means to an end. If you want to stay healthy, then you need to take some exercise.

- Morality prescribes behaviour and the Categorical Imperative gives parameters to moral law. The Categorical Imperative is not hypothetical but universal: an end in itself.

- The only actions to be followed are those that can be universalised. Suggested morals that are only right in certain circumstances are not valid and contrary to the Situationist approach. A person in distress cannot commit an act that could not be universalised, such as lying, to get out of a difficult situation. They must act as if they live in a kingdom of ends.

- Human beings should be treated as ends in themselves and not sacrificed for the good of a greater number as Utilitarians would have it.

- You must act as if you were in a kingdom of ends and not pursue moral rules that assume others are not going to behave morally.

Considering Kantian ethics

On the one hand:

- It provides a powerful set of principles to enforce moral conduct that we would commonly accept, such as condemnation of murder, rape and theft, based on reason.

- The emphasis on only treating people as ends in themselves underpins the idea of human rights, which is important today.

- Kant distinguishes duty from inclination so that our moral conduct does not become influenced by an individual subjective view as a Situationist might.

- The moral rightness or wrongness is intrinsic through a process of reason.

On the other hand:

- There might be occasions where a government needs to sacrifice an individual for the greater good. This necessary evil could not be endorsed by Kant.

- Universalisability is a good concept in principle, but as moral situations differ, how are the parameters to be set to determine what is universalised? Is there a difference between murder and self-defence? Is it murder that is universally wrong or killing in all situations?

- There may be times when duties conflict. How can these be resolved when the Categorical Imperative prohibits either being ignored?

In conclusion:

- By basing his ethics on reason, Kant avoids dependence on a 'divine' natural law, mystical Platonic Forms, or religious revelation to justify his deontological ethics.

- Kant's theory upholds the concept of human rights in a way Utilitarianism fails to do while Utilitarianism offers pragmatic solutions to the real political world.

- There are some difficulties with the internal workings of the Categorical Imperative for it to be a complete success.

Tips for AS exam questions

(a) Give an account of Kant's theory of ethics.

- You might clarify that Kantian ethics is deontological and focused on the idea of a moral law.

- You might explore the idea that moral statements are *a priori* synthetic.

- You might explore Kant's understanding of good will and duty and the link between the two.

- You could explore how moral statements are categorical and explain the workings of the Categorical Imperative with its

Names and works

Immanuel Kant, *Groundwork of the Metaphysic of Morals* (1785); *Critique of Practical Reason* (1788); *The Metaphysics of Morals* (1797)

Glossary

A priori **synthetic** Moral statements as they are known before experience through reason and yet may be right or wrong.

Categorical Imperative Only acting according to universalisable principles, treating people as ends in themselves, and acting as if you lived in a kingdom of ends.

Deontological Ethical theories that focus on acts instead of consequences.

Duty Doing only that which is approved by the Categorical Imperative out of good will.

Good will The highest good; the impetus to follow duty rather than emotion or personal inclination.

Hypothetical Imperative Acting only if a specific outcome is desired and not otherwise.

Moral law An objective moral law known through the application of reason.

universalisability; that people be considered ends in themselves and that people work towards a kingdom of ends.

(b) How helpful would this theory be when faced with the question of abortion?

- You might show how it would be difficult to universalise a view of abortion that encompasses the range of motivations and situations, as well as different stages of pregnancy at which these may occur.

- You could indicate how the requirement not to use people as a means to an end would appear to be broken if the unborn child is considered a person.

- You might consider whether sympathetic emotions should be disregarded.

- You might consider whether it is reasonable to ignore the consequences, even if they were dire, as Kant requires.

- You might like to consider whether Kant would have viewed the unborn child as a moral agent.

Critical comments

Some have argued that Kant fails to give an indication of what people should positively do as opposed to what they should not do: 'The typical examples of alleged Categorical Imperatives given by Kant tell us what not to do; not to break promises, tell lies, commit suicide, and so on. But as to what activities we ought to engage in, what ends we should pursue, the Categorical Imperative seems to be silent.' (Alasdair MacIntyre, *A Short History of Ethics*, 1967)

There is also an argument that Kant is unreasonable to place reason as the only principle on moral decision-making: given that humans may act out of compassion or love, 'the doctrine of the Categorical Imperative will really not do as an explanation of where ethics comes from. Its weakness lies in this separation of reason from all other human faculties and propensities.' (Mary Warnock, *An Intelligent Person's Guide to Ethics*, 1998)

4.2: Utilitarianism

**For the exam you
need to know about:**

- Utilitarianism: the views
of Bentham and Mill.

- The relationship between
these ethical theories and
religious methods of
ethical decision-making.

Jeremy Bentham (1748–1832)
Introduction to the Principles of Morals and Legislation (1789)

- The principle of utility – the rightness or wrongness of an action is determined by its 'utility', or usefulness, which is the amount of pleasure or happiness caused by the action.

- Utilitarianism is teleological (from the Greek word 'telos', meaning 'end') and focused on the consequences – the ends justify the means. It opposes deontological theories that focus on moral rules about acts we can or cannot do.

- Human beings seek pleasure and try to avoid pain: 'Nature has placed mankind under the governance of two sovereign masters, pain and pleasure. It is for them alone to point out what we ought to do, as well as to determine what we shall do.'

- Bentham was a hedonist in believing that pleasure is the only good and pain the only evil ('hedone' is Greek for 'pleasure'), and his theory is occasionally called hedonic Utilitarianism.

- An action is right if it produces the greatest good for the greatest number.

- The hedonic calculus provides a way of analysing and measuring the pain and pleasure of different consequences: intensity, duration, certainty or uncertainty, closeness or remoteness, the chance it has of being followed by sensations of the same kind, the purity and extent (the number affected).

- The balance of this calculation is noted and compared with the balance of pain and pleasure created by the other choices available.

John Stuart Mill
Utilitarianism (1863)

- Mill was concerned that if the greatest good for the greatest number was quantitative (based on the number of people affected and the amount of happiness rather than the nature of that happiness), nothing would stop one person's pleasure being extinguished for the majority.

- Mill replaced Bentham's quantitative measure and focused on qualitative pleasures.

- Pleasures were divided into higher and lower pleasures, preferring the higher pleasures to the lower ones: 'It is better to be a human being dissatisfied than a pig satisfied; better to be Socrates dissatisfied than a fool satisfied.'

- Pleasures of the mind are higher than those of the body and are preferred.

Act and Rule Utilitarianism

- Act Utilitarians argue that the principle of utility must be applied for each individual situation.

- We decide what is right by the value of the consequences of the act, not the act itself.

- Act Utilitarianism is flexible, taking into account individual situations.

- However, it has the potential to justify virtually any act producing extreme results and it is impractical to suggest we should measure each and every moral choice every time.

- Rule Utilitarianism establishes the best overall rule by determining the course of action, which, when pursued by the whole community, leads to the greatest result.

- This is more closely associated with John Stuart Mill (*Utilitarianism*, 1863): I must obey the rule even if it does not lead to the greatest pleasure for me in this situation. Rule Utilitarianism could still permit certain morally unacceptable practices such as slavery.

Considering Utilitarianism

On the one hand:

- It is reasonable to link morality with the pursuit of happiness and avoidance of pain and misery.

- It is a democratic morality, a commonsense, easy to grasp system designed to be practically applicable to situations.

- It is a practical theory with down-to-earth principles.

On the other hand:

- Utilitarianism relies on accurate predictions of the future, which humans do not have.

- Measuring pleasure is more complex than it suggests.

- It is questionable whether an act can be declared good by the tests of the hedonic calculus.

Names and works

Jeremy Bentham, *Introduction to the Principles of Morals and Legislation* (1789)

John Stuart Mill, *Utilitarianism* (1863)

Glossary

Act Utilitarianism The principle of utility must be directly applied for each individual situation.

Hedonic calculus Specific criteria to measure the pain and pleasure of different consequences.

Principle of utility The rightness or wrongness of an action is determined by its 'utility', or usefulness; the pleasure or happiness caused by the action.

Rule Utilitarianism The good act is the course of action, which, when pursued by the whole community, leads to the greatest result.

Teleological Ethical theories that establish the rightness or wrongness of a given act by consideration of the consequences.

Utilis Latin, meaning 'useful'.

- Alasdair MacIntyre (*A Short History of Ethics*, 1967) says Utilitarianism could justify horrendous acts as being for the pleasure of the many, such as the Nazi treatment of Jews.

- J.L. Mackie (1917–81) (*Ethics: Inventing Right and Wrong*, 1977) doubts that humans can act for the greatest good as they are often selfish.

- It is artificial to identify one's own interests with those of others as people have different tastes.

- A religious view might maintain that morality should be focused on God, not human happiness.

In conclusion:

- Modern formulations of Utilitarianism do not fully address the current concerns for justice for all including the minority issues and the issue of establishing a common view of pain and pleasure.

Tips for AS exam questions

(a) Explain the main differences between Act and Rule Utilitarianism.

- You might focus on the division among scholars between Act and Rule Utilitarianism and look at common points and main differences, with reference to key thinkers.

- You could explore Bentham's view that an act is good if it causes the greatest happiness and Mill's development of general rules of thumb and his idea of the quality of happiness rather than just quantity.

(b) To what extent is Utilitarianism a useful method of making decisions about euthanasia?

- You should show how you might apply Utilitarianism to euthanasia and appreciate its strengths and weaknesses. Whose happiness should be considered? Should anything else be considered? How would the happiness of the terminally ill be weighed against hospital staff, other sick people and the family?

- You could focus on the strengths and weaknesses of Utilitarian approaches to euthanasia. You might want to argue that another deontological or religious ethical system is preferable in dealing with life and death decisions.

- Ensure you argue a case, saying why it is useful or why it is not useful and giving reasons to justify your view.

Critical comments

Some scholars have noted that Utilitarianism allows, in theory, for us to make a slave of, or kill, an individual if it gives happiness to the majority: 'There is no *a priori* reason for thinking that the entire pleasure of one individual may be sacrificed for the greater benefit of the whole.' (Roger Scruton, *A Short History of Modern Philosophy*, 1995)

'What application has [Utilitarianism] in a society where the public happiness is found by the public itself to consist in the mass murder of Jews?' (Alasdair MacIntyre, *A Short History of Ethics*, 1967)

Others have felt it over-simplifies or distorts happiness: 'Hedonism misunderstands the nature of happiness. Happiness is not something that is recognised as good and sought for its own sake with other things appreciated only as a means of bringing it about. Instead, happiness is a response we have to the attainment of things that we recognise as good.' (James Rachels, *The Elements of Moral Philosophy*, 1986)

4.3: Absolute and relative morality

For the exam you need to know about:

- The concepts of absolute and relative morality.

- The relationship between these ethical theories and religious methods of ethical decision-making.

Absolute morality

- An absolute is a moral command/prohibition that is objectively/universally true.

- Actions are right or wrong intrinsically (deontologically) – consequences or circumstances have no bearing.

- Plato believed that moral absolutes, such as goodness and justice, really existed beyond the world in an eternal state and called them Forms or Ideals.

- Aquinas argued that one could 'follow the good and avoid the evil' and suggested that the moral way of living is to do that which is objectively good and avoid that which is objectively bad.

- Aquinas' Natural Law is absolutist – certain acts are intrinsically right or wrong depending on whether they are in accordance with the laws of God, found within nature. The Roman Catholic Church today applies this to certain acts, such as the use of artificial contraception, which it considers intrinsically evil.

- Christian absolutists tend to measure right or wrong in absolute terms: 'Our approach is that universal biblical norms are absolute.' (Robertson McQuilkin)

Relative morality

- Some societies hold that it is acceptable for a man to marry more than one wife while others feel that such a practice is a crime. Different cultures express different moral codes.

- Aristotle believed that Plato was wrong about the Forms being eternal and beyond this world. He argued that they were within this world and could change from place to place.

- People participate in different ways of living because they actually follow different codes.

- Modern anthropologists have observed cultural differences in morality and some have concluded that the existence of diverse moral codes implies only 'socially approved habits'.

- Anthropologist William Graham Sumner (1840–1910) (*Folkways*, 1906) said, 'The "right" way is the way which the ancestors used and which has been handed down.' Moral rules are expressions of the culture.

- Some moral relativists hold that no one moral system can be valued above another. Subjectivists, such as Ayer, argue that moral statements are purely emotive expressions with no value beyond saying 'hurrah' or 'boo'. They express emotional objection of attachment to ideas.

Considering moral relativism and absolutism
Strengths of moral relativism

- Moral relativists appreciate cultural and religious differences and understand their importance.

- It explains the existence of different moral codes as diverse cultural expressions.

- It prohibits a dominant culture imposed imperialistically.

- It is flexible and accommodates different lifestyles.

Weaknesses of moral relativism

- 'One should not regard all the opinions that people hold, but only some and not others…One should regard the good ones and not the bad.' (Socrates) Not all views are equally true.

- It cannot criticise a culture or condemn practices that might be accepted by society (such as wife beating, which used to be accepted in English history) because there is no objective measure to judge them.

- It reduces 'good' to 'socially approved' or personally preferred.

- If the relative belief that differing moral codes should all be supported was adopted universally, relativism itself would become an absolute moral code!

Strengths of absolutism

- Absolutism provides a fixed code to measure actions.

- It can condemn what relativists find difficult to do so: Nazi Germany or the wife-beater, for example.

Names and works

Aristotle, *Nicomachean Ethics* (4th century BCE)

J.L. Mackie, *Ethics: Inventing Right and Wrong* (1977)

Plato, *The Republic* (4th century BCE)

Glossary

Absolutism The belief that there are ethical absolutes or objective moral norms and moral rules that are true for all time and places; that acts are right or wrong in themselves.

Cultural relativism The belief that cultural practices are ethically equal or that there is no way of reaching an objective standpoint by which they can be judged.

Subjectivism The view that morality is subjective and 'true' for the individual.

- It gives moral guidelines to reinforce a global perspective.

- One country may judge the actions of another country as wrong and act on that judgement.

- The United Nations Declaration of Human Rights suggests a set of absolutes that apply to all people, regardless of where they live.

- Cultures seem to have common beliefs regarding the treatment of children, which are rationally demonstrable.

Weaknesses of absolutism

- It cannot consider circumstances of the situation or consequences of the action.

- Absolutism can seem intolerant of cultural diversity in the way in which European nations were in the past.

Tips for AS exam questions

(a) Explain the differences between a relative morality and an absolute one.

- You might contrast the idea of there being fixed moral norms for all people with the idea that they might vary from person to person/culture to culture or situation to situation, and you could give examples of how a moral act might be treated in broad terms by each.

- You might consider ideas such as universality and truth with the idea that moral truth is obscure or impossible to identify.

- You might consider forms of relativism such as Situationism and absolutism such as Natural Law, and how they would differ in their approach to a moral dilemma.

(b) How useful is a relative morality in dealing with issues surrounding genetic engineering?

- You might like to illustrate how having different moral rules makes it difficult to legislate on issues such as human cloning (reproductive or therapeutic), genetic modification of crops or animals, and stem cell research.

- Is the consequence of having a relative morality a slippery slope, as no single act would be wrong forever or in all places, so ultimately all ideas would come to fruition?

- You could argue that a relative morality might be able to change as a better understanding of the science became more clear while absolute moralities might be left irrelevant when they are no longer upheld by the science.

Critical comments

The idea that there are clear knowable objective moral truths has been challenged by anthropologists: 'Influenced by Darwinian theory, early anthropological theory tended to arrange the peoples and social institutions of the world in an evolutionary series, from primordial man to the civilised human being of nineteenth-century Europe. Many anthropologists eventually reacted against the imperialism of their government…More importantly, they came to see the peoples they studied as intelligent men and women whose lives had meaning and integrity. And this led to questioning the basis for implicit judgements of the inferiority of their ways of life, especially after the spectacle of the civilised nations in brutal struggle with one another in the First World War.' (David Wong, in *A Companion to Ethics*, 1997)

4.4: Abortion

For the exam you need to know about:

- Practical ethics – theory as applied to medical ethics: abortion.

- The ways in which the ethical systems of Natural Law, Virtue Ethics, Kant, Bentham and Mill might be raised by these areas.

- Religious responses to these issues.

The right to life

- The idea of human rights dates back to Stoic beliefs but has been reinforced in the Universal Declaration of Human Rights. They imply that humans have inalienable rights, including protection from certain actions. They express a deontological and absolute view.

- Rights can be linked to a divine law (Natural Law) or rationality with Kant's idea that humans must be treated as ends in themselves. There is a presumed right to life, though exceptions are made in warfare and the death penalty.

- Sometimes the rights given to humans are given in a limited way to unborn humans at certain stages of development, but the unborn human is rarely considered to be an equal under the law.

- Throughout the world, the right to life is conditional on the nature and status of that life. Often presented as an absolute, it needs a basis, be it a Platonic absolute, humanitarian obligation, demand of reason, or divine command.

- Throughout the world, rights differ as they depend on community recognition and communities differ – although protection of the innocent does seem a fundamental value in many cultures.

- Feminists argue that the right over their reproductive system is a fundamental right without which women cannot live in liberty.

- The right to life argument, taken to the extreme, gives the unborn child equality with the mother and yet in practice the mother is given priority over the unborn child, especially if dependents are involved.

The sanctity of life

- No biblical text specifically prohibits abortion, though some Christians argue that a number of verses suggest it (for example, Genesis 4.1; Isaiah 44.24, 48.1; Jeremiah 1.5; Luke 1.40, 42).

- Human life is sacred, implying respect. Religious arguments against abortion stress the limits of human authority over the taking of life. God is the life-creator and giver, and humans must not destroy what God has given.

- Many religions reject the taking of innocent life and that includes abortion. The Roman Catholic Church maintains that it is intrinsically evil and condemns it absolutely.

- Abortion goes against Natural Law and some interpretations of the biblical Word of God, and there are no exceptions or scenarios that make it right. The foetus deserves the same status as a born human being.

- Some liberal Christians oppose abortion in principle, and advocate the preservation of life, but allow it in certain situations such as where the mother's life is threatened.

- Christianity holds that life is sacred and deserves respect as it is created by God and in God's image. Taking life is intrinsically evil and against the commandments. Some argue the unborn human life should be protected as God alone is Lord of life. Humans have no authority to take life.

- In Natural Law, preserving the innocent is a primary precept.

- Capital punishment and killing in war can be justified with reference to consequences or desperate situations. Acceptance of such killing, which obviously rejects the idea of the intrinsic value of life, is at odds with such an attitude against abortion.

- The idea of sacred rests on religious beliefs, which atheists contest, though it arguably captures a defining feature of humanity, which is supported by a secular spirituality or humanitarian ethic.

Personhood

- Should life be protected from the moment of conception or should status increase incrementally as the foetus develops?

- From the Catholic perspective, Pope Pius IX declared that a foetus is a human person from the moment of conception and so abortion is always murder. Others argue that the ovum is too different from anything we would recognise as a person to be treated as the same.

- Some writers think that there is continuous development in foetal growth but suggest that there is a point at which it is not a human being. There is a continuous growth from acorn to oak tree, but an acorn is not an oak tree, just as a fertilised ovum, a newly implanted clump of cells, is not a person.

Glossary

Personhood The state in which a living being has moral rights and responsibilities, and is usually thought of as a self-conscious, sentient being.

Rights Usually protections or powers that humans have under the law.

Sanctity A holy or sacred thing; 'of God'; something precious and of value.

Viable The stage of development when a foetus can survive outside the womb.

- Some argue that birth marks the beginning of true moral status and a foetus is not a person, as sperm and ovum are not persons. Jonathan Glover rejects this because of the similarity between later foetuses and premature babies.

- A foetus may be a person when it is viable but is a foetus as much of a 'person' as a baby, which needs a lot of support and protection to survive?

- Personhood could be defined by consciousness, rationality, self-awareness or language, but there is no agreement over this, so personhood is not a good basis for a moral absolute.

- Ambiguities over the definition of personhood may strengthen the case against abortion. The precautionary principle says that in the absence of certainty about the start of the human person, we should choose the point of conception.

- On the other hand, it may weaken the case against abortion on the basis that the disputable status of personhood does not provide firm evidence to prohibit abortion. The human being just after conception is demonstrably not the same as the born human being. A line may be drawn for the giving of full rights only when more recognisable human features exist.

- Self-consciousness or self-awareness cannot define personhood, as very young babies are not self-aware in the fullest sense, and most would argue that killing babies is murder.

Tips for AS exam questions

(a) What is Virtue Ethics?

- You might consider Aristotle's idea about virtues and the virtuous mean and how this approach is a person-centred one.

- You could consider MacIntyre's approach to the virtues as a modern version of the theory.

- You might explore the idea of person-centred ethics rather than act- or end-focused ethics, with the rightness/wrongness being measured by how virtuous the people are or become.

(b) Discuss the view that it is never virtuous to obtain an abortion.

- You could explore the idea of being virtuous and consider what its foundations are and whether it is the exclusive moral consideration in any action.

- You might explore in some detail how the outcomes of an abortion may or may not be virtuous.

- You may consider the virtues of the medical staff involved.

- You might like to consider whether all outcomes would make for virtuous living or whether some outcomes should be avoided.

Critical comments

Mrs Jill Knight, MP, 1966, in a House of Commons debate (in Glover, 1977), said: 'Babies are not like bad teeth to be jerked out just because they cause suffering. An unborn baby is a baby nevertheless. Would the sponsors of the bill think it right to kill a baby they can see? Of course they would not. Why then do they think it right to kill one they cannot see?…Uninterfered with, it has a potential life ahead of it of 70 years or more; it may be a happy one, or a sad life; it may be a genius, or it may be just plain average; but surely as a healthy, living baby it has a right not to be killed simply because it may be inconvenient for a year or so to its mother.'

4.5: Euthanasia

For the exam you need to know about:

- Practical ethics – theory as applied to medical ethics: euthanasia.

- The ways in which the ethical systems of Natural Law, Virtue Ethics, Kant, Bentham and Mill might be raised by these areas.

- Religious responses to these issues.

- For this topic you need to be aware of issues and arguments concerning the right to life/sanctity of life, which are covered in the previous unit.

- For someone who has led a full and active life but is now suffering from an incurable disease that slowly limits their abilities, euthanasia appears to offer an opportunity for them to choose the manner and timing of their death with dignity.

- Is it the same as suicide and should a doctor be allowed to help? How can the quality of someone's life be measured and compared? What if they cannot express their will themselves?

- Euthanasia is a criminal offence in virtually all countries and it is strongly opposed by most governments and religious organisations. In Holland, about a thousand assisted deaths take place each year. Organisations, such as the Voluntary Euthanasia Society (VES), campaign for a similar practice to be available in the UK.

- The Greek philosopher Hippocrates (5th century BCE) wrote: 'I will not prescribe a deadly drug to please someone, nor give advice that may cause his death.' Does care for the patient include helping them to end their life?

- Francis Bacon (1561–1626) wrote that physicians are 'not only to restore the health, but to mitigate pain and dolours [distress]; and not only when such mitigation may conduce to recovery, but when it may serve to make a fair and easy passage.' ('New Atlantis', 1627)

Arguments for voluntary euthanasia

- Voluntary euthanasia is not murder – it is not wrong to help the dying to die because they are already dying.

- Voluntary euthanasia shows mercy for those suffering with intolerable pain from an incurable disease.

- Voluntary euthanasia gives people autonomy; some control over their own life.

- Euthanasia occurs already as doctors can legally give pain-relieving treatment in doses that will bring about people's deaths more quickly, and, in certain circumstances, such as the case of the brain-dead or comatose, they may also withdraw or withhold treatment even though the person will die. Those arguing for voluntary euthanasia would say this should be extended to all who wish to end their lives.

- Voluntary euthanasia maintains quality of life by allowing the end of life to be dignified.

Religious arguments against voluntary euthanasia

- In general terms, Christianity, Islam, Judaism and Buddhism oppose euthanasia, including voluntary euthanasia, while Sikhism and Hinduism tend to leave it to the individual's conscience.

- In many religious traditions, life is a sacred gift from God, which should be preserved and not attacked.

- Killing is forbidden. In the Hebrew scriptures (also considered the Christian Old Testament), the sixth commandment states: 'Thou shalt not commit murder.' The Quran says, 'Take not life which Allah made sacred otherwise than in the course of justice' (Qur'an 6.151), and, 'Do not kill (or destroy) yourselves, for verily Allah has been to you most Merciful.' (Qur'an 4.29)

Other arguments against euthanasia

- Doubtful motives – we cannot be sure that a person who asks for death is fully informed, not going to rethink, not under perceived pressures, which may or may not exist, from society, friends or the medical profession.

- Can we be sure that mistakes will not occur? Someone could choose death after a misdiagnosis.

- There is the possibility that the system could be manipulated or abused.

- Allowing euthanasia might have negative cultural affects on society, with people accepting death as a form of treatment, creating possible fears for those going to hospital, and reducing respect for life.

- The argument of an individual's right to die must be set against the community in which individuals exist.

Evaluating voluntary euthanasia

- Is there a moral difference between the withdrawal of treatment (legal in the UK) and the active killing of a patient by a lethal injection?

Glossary

Assisted suicide When another person, possibly a doctor, assists someone to end their life.

Euthanasia Literally meaning 'a good death'; taking the life of someone who is terminally ill.

Hippocratic Oath The oath doctors take promising to heal the sick.

Voluntary euthanasia A person freely choosing to end their own life themselves.

- The religious arguments against voluntary euthanasia carry the weight of theological and teaching traditions, which some challenge or reject altogether.

- Many arguments in the debate relate to consequences about which we cannot be certain.

- We cannot predict the impact that voluntary euthanasia might have on people's perceptions of hospitals or how it might affect an elderly person's perception of whether he or she is a burden to others.

- Prohibiting voluntary euthanasia is a restriction on individual autonomy – but would there be wider social dangers if this restriction was lifted?

Tips for AS exam questions

(a) Give an account of Kant's theory of ethics.

- You might clarify that Kantian ethics is deontological and focused on the idea of a moral law.

- You might explore the idea that moral statements are *a priori* synthetic.

- You might explore Kant's understanding of good will and duty and the link between the two.

- You could explore how moral statements are categorical and explain the workings of the Categorical Imperative with its universalisability; that people be considered ends in themselves and that people work towards a kingdom of ends.

(b) How helpful would this theory be when faced with the problem of dying without dignity?

- Focus on the specifics of the question and the application of the principle rather than the background to euthanasia.

- You could explain that the Categorical Imperative creates universalisable moral rules, which make it impossible to react according to the situation.

- Universalisability might mean no euthanasia is ever permissible or that it would be always permissible for any reason, unless specific circumstances could be defined and universalised.

- There is a conflict between universalisability and acting out of compassion. It is also unclear how a person wanting their own death might be treated, considering them as an end in themselves.

Critical comments

The idea that life is sacred is used by religious groups to argue against euthanasia, abortion and other crimes against human life. The Roman Catholic Church condemns crimes against life, 'such as any type of murder, genocide, abortion, euthanasia, or wilful suicide.' Life is sacred and a gift from God, 'which they are called upon to preserve and make fruitful.' (Pastoral Constitution, *Gaudium et Spes*, No. 27, and *Declaration on Euthanasia*, 1980)

The *Islamic Code of Medical Ethics* (Islamic Organisation of Medical Sciences, 1981) states the following: 'Mercy killing, like suicide, finds no support except in the atheistic way of thinking that our life on this earth is followed by void. The claim of killing for painful, hopeless illness is also refuted, for there is no human pain that cannot be largely conquered by medication or by suitable neurosurgery.'

4.6: Genetic engineering, embryo research and the right to a child

For the exam you need to know about:

- Practical ethics – theory as applied to medical ethics: genetic engineering, embryo research and the right to a child.

- The ways in which the ethical systems of Natural Law, Virtue Ethics, Kant, Bentham and Mill might be raised by these areas.

- Religious responses to these issues.

- For this topic you need to be aware of issues and arguments concerning the right to life/sanctity of life; refer to Unit 4.4 for this.

Genetic engineering

- Genetic engineering is the alteration of genetic code by artificial means. This covers a wide area, including many legal, medical and religious ethical issues. One area of controversy, for example, is the genetic modification of crops, which may be seen as 'meddling' with God's creation – or helping to solve recurring famine in developing countries. Many debates currently focus on human cloning, and this is the topic we will consider here.

- Human cloning is the creation of an embryo using the genetic material from another human being so that it is an identical copy.

- The technology could help couples who cannot conceive. Therapeutic cloning can help to cure inherited genetic disorders or conditions that damage the human body's specialised cell parts, such as Alzheimer's disease and Parkinson's disease.

- Some argue that full human rights status is given from conception and the embryo is sacred (created by God, with a destiny given by God and in God's image) and so the removal of an embryo's nucleus is the destruction of a unique being.

- Some argue that cloning is acceptable only for embryo research and cloned beings should not be allowed to develop. There is an argument that human cloning raises no new ethical questions as identical twins share more properties than cloned humans.

- There are a number of potential consequential benefits, such as giving children to childless couples and the curing of degenerative diseases. On the other hand, there is a possibility of psychological and/or emotional damage for cloned beings and society's attitude to reproduction could be eroded.

- It could be argued that it is inevitable that human cloning will happen somewhere in the world, so a pragmatic approach should be taken.

Embryo research

- Embryo experimentation has the potential of finding cures for serious illnesses by using tissue or cells from embryos.

- UK politicians voted to extend the research done on human embryos to allow stem cells to be taken from embryos at a very early stage of development in the hope that this may lead to radical improvements in the treatment of a number of degenerative diseases.

- Embryo experimentation and research may bring benefits for the greater good through possible greater benefits, which may come from the sacrifice of the embryo.

- There are a number of dimensions to the debate, including the storage of embryos, whether they should be stored for long periods of time, and how they are 'disposed' of afterwards.

- Important to this discussion is the nature of the embryo and whether it is a person, a potential person, or something else, and whether and to what degree rights are given.

- The British Humanist Association note that before fourteen days an embryo has few human characteristics, although others argue that at day seven there are observable features.

- Some Christian absolutists argue for full rights from the point of conception because any interruption in the process of life interrupts God's plan for life.

- Others argue against potentiality as an argument as sperm and eggs could not be considered potentially human.

- Religious absolutists with strong pro-life beliefs see the use of embryos in this way as an indicator of a totalitarian society that thinks it can use and abuse individual humans for utilitarian reasons.

- There is a danger of making human beings into a commodity, something to be utilised for the good of others (Utilitarianism) over and against any unique untouchable status that they might have.

- Whether or not an embryo is a person fundamentally affects the view of IVF and embryo research.

The right to a child

- Infertile couples have the chance of having assisted reproductive technologies (for example, IVF), which requires many embryos as the process usually requires more than one attempt for success.

- Unused embryos are kept in frozen storage and are eventually destroyed.

- Some argue that infertility is a condition that can be treated and that people have a right to receive such treatment to have children that are biologically theirs.

- Others argue that the destruction of the unused embryos is the destruction of sacred life, which outweighs the desire for children.

- A child is another human being and ordinarily we do not have rights to have another human being. Christian absolutists who believe in the sanctity of life object to assisted reproductive technologies.

Tips for AS exam questions

(a) Explain how the principals of Natural Law might be applied to decisions about fertility treatment.

- You could outline your understanding of genetic engineering, and the ethical issues surrounding it, and of Natural Law's position. IVF, for example, necessarily involves the destruction of embryos. Natural Law requires that the life of the innocent be protected. If an unborn human embryo is treated as one of these innocent lives, then both practices break a primary precept and cannot be allowed.

- You could explain that Natural Law is absolutist and deontological and how it cannot allow any consideration of the benefits for the greater good from research or by creating more life by helping infertility.

- You could explore the issue of whether an embryo is considered a human person.

- Natural Law depends upon the outcome of the debate about personhood and is therefore limited in its effectiveness.

(b) 'Every adult has the right to become a parent.' Discuss.

- You could explore the idea of whether we have a right to another person, whether this makes human life a commodity, whether we simply have duties to other people, especially those whom we bring up.

- Some couples who are unable to have children suffer greatly as a result: you could explore how medical advances that allowed them to have children would greatly improve their lives.

Glossary

AI Artificial insemination: the putting of sperm into a female by means of an instrument to achieve fertilisation.

IVF *In vitro* fertilisation: a procedure in which sperm are placed with an unfertilised egg in a Petri dish to achieve fertilisation.

Stem cells Special cells found in embryos that have distinctive properties and can lead to specialised cells.

Therapeutic cloning The nuclear transplantation of a patient's own cells to make a cell from which immune-compatible cells can be derived for transplant.

- You could explore the argument that reproductive technologies are too costly for every childless couple to have as many treatments may be required for them to conceive; resources for this would have to be taken from other areas of medicine, which could cost lives.

Critical comments

Genetic engineering, IVF and embryo research raise issues about how we value human life: 'That way lies the moral approach of a totalitarian society, that thinks it can use and abuse individual human beings in accordance with some grand scheme promising "the greatest good for the greatest number"...If, as modern embryology tells us...[genetically defective embryos]...are indeed part of the continuum of human life, then the notion that genetic flaws enable us to destroy the "imperfect" embryos has implications for the equal dignity of human beings after birth as well.' (Richard Doerflinger, responding for the National Conference of Catholic Bishops at a PBS Newshour forum (Ref. 6), quoted by the Ontario Consultants on Religious Tolerance, www.religious tolerance.org)

5.1: The body and soul

For the exam you need to know about:

• The body/soul distinction in the thinking of Plato, John Hick and Richard Dawkins.

Introduction

• Materialism is the view that the mind cannot be separated from the body.

• Idealism is the view that the mind is the only reality and the body is unreal.

• Dualism is the view that the mind and body both exist and are linked in some way.

Plato

• Review Plato's distinction between body and soul in the foundation unit so that you can make comparisons with the thinking of Hick and of Dawkins.

John Hick
Philosophy of Religion (1973)*; Death and Eternal Life* (1976)

• The soul is a name for the moral, spiritual self formed by the interaction of genes and environment. The human is a psychophysical person with a divine purpose.

• The person shall be resurrected through a divine act of recreation or reconstitution in resurrection, rather than reincarnation as Plato would have it, through God's creative love.

• The new body is not the old one brought back to life but a spiritual body inhabiting a spiritual world just as the physical body inhabited a physical world.

• Hick conducts a thought experiment with a hypothetical person called John Smith. Smith disappears from the USA and reappears in Calcutta, India. He is physically identical with the same memories, emotions, fingerprints, and so on. People would agree he was Smith. If he died and reappeared in this world, again identical, people would agree he was Smith. If he died and reappeared in another world with other resurrected people, he would be Smith. This is called the replica theory.

- God is not restricted by death and holds man beyond natural mortality.

- Luther wrote: 'Anyone with whom God speaks, whether in wrath or mercy, the same is certainly immortal.'

Richard Dawkins
The Selfish Gene (1976); *River out of Eden* (1986); *The Blind Watchmaker* (1995)

- Dawkins the evolutionist argues that humans are merely carriers of DNA, 'just bytes and bytes of digital information.' Information flows through time, the bones and tissues do not.

- The belief in an immortal soul is anachronistic and damaging to human endeavor. There is 'no spirit-driven life force, no throbbing, heaving, pullulating, protoplasmic, mystic jelly.'

- Dawkins argues that myths (such as Plato's Forms) and faiths are not supported by evidence; scientific beliefs are. Life lacks purpose and is indifferent to suffering. There is no creator God.

- Evolution is the only rational theory. It is not our soul that guides us but our genetic make-up. Over time, the good genes survive and the bad genes die out.

- We are as we are because of our genetic make-up, not the efforts of our soul to guide us towards the realm of Ideas. No soul continues, only DNA, the function of life.

- Our sense of self and individuality is based on digital information, not the soul. Our genes are a colony of information that wants to be replicated. It is easier for this to happen in a multi-cell organism. 'We are survival machines – robot vehicles blindly programmed to preserve the selfish molecules known as genes.' (*The Selfish Gene*, 1976)

- The genes are found in behaviour, so the bodies acquire individuality. We feel like a single organism, not a colony, as selection has favoured genes that co-operate.

- Genes working together give us a sense of individuality, not the soul. The colony needs a central control. The genetic model becomes more complex and thinks about itself as an individual and considers the consequences of its actions.

- 'Consciousness arises when the brain's simulation of the world becomes so complete that it must include a model of itself.' (*The Selfish Gene*, 1976)

- This leads to human culture, a 'replicator' or 'meme' (tunes, catchphrases, quotes, teachings), which are heard and lodged in the brain and then imitated by it.

- At death, we leave behind genes and memes, though the genes will quickly be dispersed. DNA survival brings about the body and individual consciousness creates culture. This is the soul.

Debates about the body/soul distinction

- Aquinas believed the soul animated the body and gave it life. The soul is the anima, the source of all activity. It survives death taking the identity of its body.

- Descartes rejected the naturalistic idea that the soul gave life to the body and when it left the body died. He thought the relation of the soul with the body came from the connection that we could move our bodies and also that we could experience changes on or in our bodies.

- The body is corporeal, the mind non-corporeal. The mind is where thoughts and feelings are known and the body performs physical actions.

- We do not move the body as a mind steering a ship. The soul/mind is united with the body. The soul is joined to all parts of the body and informs it. We know that the mind is affected by things we do to the body, especially chemical abuse. When we die, the soul moves on to God.

- Descartes also maintained that the body and soul were complete substances leading to a tension between that and the idea the body is not steered by the soul.

- Hick argues that there is evidence of the existence of a spiritual aspect of the person that may be found in parapsychology, such as ESP, telepathy, clairvoyance, apparitions, séances, reincarnation memories, out of body experiences (OOBE), near-death experiences (NDE), and so on.

- The evidence is not conclusive, though it is wrong to take absence of knowledge to mean knowledge of absence. It is not irrational to believe the self survives death in the soul. A personal survival is a necessary condition for immortality.

- Some religious texts talk about the soul, which would be an argument for a religious believer that they exist on the basis of the authority of these sacred texts.

- If a person believes in God, then it naturally extends, according to Hick, that souls exist. It is contradictory for

Names and works

Richard Dawkins, *The Selfish Gene* (1976); *River out of Eden* (1986); *The Blind Watchmaker* (1995)

John Hick, *Philosophy of Religion* (1973); *Death and Eternal Life* (1976)

Glossary

Anima Aquinas' view of the soul; the source of all activity.

Memes A replicator of human culture, which is passed on.

Replica theory Hick's theory that if a person vanished and a replica appeared in another world, people would presume that that person was the same person.

God to create people to live in fellowship with God if they are limited.

- Perry (*A Dialogue on Personal Identity and Immortality*, 1978) argues that souls cannot establish a personal identity since souls are immaterial. Whether or not any souls exist, or have ever existed, they are unobservable and could never be testable. There is no evidence that it is the same personal identity. Even if the soul had passed from one temporal form to another in the afterlife, only divine inspiration could tell for sure.

- Perry also argues against those who use memory as evidence. A being in the next world may have a memory of being in the first, but memory can be misleading or even false and cannot be relied upon.

- Gilbert Ryle (1900–76) (*The Concept of Mind*, 1949) argues that we make a categorical mistake by thinking that the noun 'soul' refers to a concrete object in the way that the noun 'body' does.

- The soul does not exist as a separate thing, in the same way the spirit in 'team spirit' does not exist in a separate way.

- Ryle opposed the dualist separation between a tangible body and an intangible mind or soul. All references to the mental must be understood in terms of witnessable activities. The body/soul distinction is a myth and scientifically literate people have no use of it. The soul is a name for the set of properties or dispositions of the person.

- Hegel (1770–1831) argued that the mind imposes order on the senses and so we cannot be certain of any physical objects. Our souls come from the underlying universal soul. History is the development of the spirit through time.

Tips for A2 exam questions

'The body/soul distinction is a myth invented by philosophers such as Plato.' Discuss.

- Explain the distinction formulated by Plato and his belief in an immortal soul and reincarnation. The soul contemplates the Forms between incarnations. The distinction expresses a belief in life beyond the physical demise of the body.

- One approach could be to explain that Christian beliefs in the soul, as expressed by people such as Hick, do not encompass reincarnation but do hold that the soul moves on to live beyond this world. Reference could be made to Descartes' view of the soul.

- Hick's evidence of supernatural events could be considered as evidence.

- Hick's reasoning that in principle the soul could exist beyond this world should be explored as well as the religious reasons for belief in the soul once belief in God was accepted.

- Dawkins' alternative explanation of the sense of personal identity could be considered.

Critical comments

Dawkins rejects any idea of a soul that lives beyond death: 'When we die, there are two things we can leave behind us: genes and memes. We were built as gene machines, created to pass on our genes, but that aspect of us will be forgotten in three generations. Your child, even your grandchild, may bear a passing resemblance to you, perhaps in a talent for music, in the colour of her hair. But as each generation passes, the contribution of your genes is halved. It does not take long to reach negligible proportions. Our genes may be immortal but the collection of genes which is any one of us is bound to crumble away. Elizabeth II is a direct descendent of William the Conqueror, yet it is quite probable that she bears not a single one of the old king's genes. We should seek immortality in reproduction, but if you contribute to the world's culture, if you have a good idea, or compose a tune, invent a sparking plug, write a poem, it may live on intact, long after your genes have dissolved in the common pool.' (Richard Dawkins, *The Selfish Gene*, 1976)

5.2: Life after death

For the exam you need to know about:
- Different views of life after death, resurrection and rebirth.
- The implications for the problem of evil of these views.

Introduction

Life may be disembodied (separate from the body) as Plato argued, leaving the body to corrupt on earth, or life continues in some bodily form. Peter Geach, a contemporary British philosopher, writes, 'Apart from the possibility of resurrection, it seems to me a mere illusion to have any hope for life after death. I am of the mind of Judas Maccabeus: if there is no resurrection, it is superfluous and vain to pray for the dead.'

Disembodied survival after death

- Descartes, Lewis and Swinburne are dualists arguing that we exist beyond our bodies. If people are distinct from their bodies, then after death they exist in a disembodied state. Descartes thought this was possible.

- H.D. Lewis argues that we detect mental processes quite distinct from physical ones, suggesting a non-physical self. Richard Swinburne argues that people could conceivably not be limited to using a chunk of matter for perception, knowledge and control.

- Descartes argues that the body is divisible, parts can be severed, but the mind is not. We conceive ourselves as separate from the body. Yet while Descartes may feel he cannot divide his mind, it is not proof that it cannot be done.

- Descartes argues that he can doubt his body but not that he exists. Norman Malcolm argues against Descartes, suggesting that if Descartes were right, we could doubt that a thinking being exists, but that would not imply we were not thinking beings.

- Swinburne argues that it is coherent to describe someone as disembodied, although Brian Davies questions whether we conceive ourselves as disembodied. To live means to participate in activities, which requires a body.

Bodily survival after death

- While it may be possible for me to conceive of life in a new bodily form, it does not mean I actually will have life with a new bodily form.

- Hick argues for the possibility of replica bodies (see Unit 5.1). Brian Davies argues that he would not be content to receive a lethal injection on the basis that a replica with identical memories, feelings, thoughts and physique would exist.

- John Locke (1632–1704) argued that the body is distinct from the person. A person is a thinking, intelligent being with reason and reflection. A person can exist in a spiritual world and can move from body to body.

- Brian Davies argues that it might be the case that after death we continue as a being that is physically continuous with what has died.

Resurrection and rebirth

- Resurrection is a belief held by Christians that the body, a spiritual body, will rise again after its death. The 'I' that lives now will rise again and be identifiable in the afterlife.

- The Christian Gospels state that Jesus rose from the dead. St Paul considers this fundamental to Christianity – proof both of Jesus' identity and that God's plan will come to fruition.

- Jesus said those who believed in him would have eternal life. St Paul described the new life as being with spiritual bodies. The Nicene and Apostle's Creeds both confirm the resurrection of the body.

- Rebirth is a common idea in Eastern religions. There is continuity from one life to another. The body dies but the person lives a different life in a new body. The nature of the new life is determined by the law of karma, by what was done by the person in the previous life.

- In Hindu belief, the atman (soul) moves from body to body until it becomes the one spirit or undifferentiated consciousness.

- Buddhists hold that the life of the person is connected through the law of karma to another life, although the soul as such does not exist. The process is linked and the individuality that a person feels is related to the process and context. This life is determined by our acts in the last life.

The concept of Heaven and Hell

- In the New Testament, Heaven is a place with God where good people go when they die after the Day of Judgement.

Names and works

René Descartes, *Meditations on First Philosophy* (1641)

John Hick, *Philosophy of Religion* (1973); *Death and Eternal Life* (1976)

Norman Malcolm, 'Descartes' Proof that his Essence is Thinking,' in *Descartes* (1968)

- Roman Catholic theology sees eternal life as a timeless Beatific Vision of God. On death, the person goes to Heaven, Hell or Purgatory.

- The New Testament speaks of God's wrath and punishment. In Matthew 25, the unrighteous are sent to the 'eternal fire' on the Day of Judgement. Parables say that no-one can return from this place.

- Hick argues that the idea of Hell is something that humanity could achieve on earth without the need for a reality in the next world. However, if Hell is not to be interpreted literally, why not treat Heaven similarly?

- Hick also argues that one could conceive of another place that is no distance or direction from me. There could be many of these other worlds.

- Hell may be viewed less literally and taken as the suffering of this life. A contemporary way for viewing Hell is a person determined to freely turn away from God after death. God will not force someone to God.

- Purgatory is a place of cleansing of the soul; a temporal punishment for lesser sins before Heaven. A contemporary view of Purgatory is the journey from selfishness to selflessness. Heaven is the timeless and completely satisfying vision of God.

Is it reasonable to believe in life after death?

- Some evidence put forward is parapsychological (or psychical), such as near-death experiences, mediums, and so on, though the data generated from such evidence is contested.

- Plato argues that life is opposite to death. Death comes from life, so logically life must come from death otherwise all would end up dead and there would be no life. However, life and death are not attributes to be acquired.

- Descartes argues that the human person/self is not divisable, not identified with the body, and continues after the body. However, there is no reason to suppose only things that have parts will die.

- Kant's moral argument for the existence of God is also an argument for life after death. However, some dispute the existence of a moral imperative.

- Arguably, morality could make sense without the need for life after death as it would bring about a better world.

Some people argue that their faith is a reason for believing in life after death.

- Most people do not remember anything of previous lives, undermining the argument for the soul from memory. On the other hand, some claim to recover memories from a previous life through hypnosis, though this cannot be tested empirically.

- Hick says that memory is important evidence for the continuity of the same person. If memory is wiped at rebirth, then how can we be sure it is the same person?

- The body is different, and possibly also the memory. The only comparable aspect is character or dispositions, but there are many broad similarities between hundreds of thousands of people living now and many hundreds of thousands of people living previously. This, too, does not provide solid evidence.

- Modern physics denies the possibility of resurrection. It seems scientifically implausible that God could resurrect the disintegrated body. However, this objection ignores the idea that the body is a spiritual body, a new body.

- Is belief in life after death an answer to the problem of evil? It seems unjust that people are moral, have a hard life and die with no reward. The possibility of judgement and Hell vindicates the good and punishes the bad. However, the matter of natural evil is not addressed by this possibility and it could be argued that the suffering is not worth the prize of Heaven. Also, it does not explain why suffering seems to be so arbitrary – are people who happen to have good fortune and comfortable lives going to receive less after death through no fault of their own?

- The concept of karma, from Eastern religions, seems to justify the evil and suffering in the world. It is down to the actions of that person in a previous life. However, when the person suffering cannot remember that past life, or is too young to understand the philosophy of karma, questions might be asked as to whether the system is fair. In Hinduism, though, the question of fairness does not arise as the results of karma are not 'reward' or 'punishment', they are just the results of your own actions according to the eternal laws of the universe.

Tips for A2 exam questions

'It is impossible to justify innocent suffering unless there is life after death.' Discuss.

- Explain how the existence of the suffering of the innocent, be it through natural or human evil, seems unjust.

- The doctrine of original sin could be explored as a form of justification, or the argument of karma, though the limitations of these ideas should also be explored.

- The traditional theodicies could be explored, in which the suffering is argued to have a purpose, enabling the individual to mature and to exercise free will, with consideration both to Augustine and Irenaeus.

- The extent of suffering, citing extreme cases such as genocide and child starvation, and the fact that it seems arbitrary, could be contrasted with the view of Hick that everything will be revealed and put right after death in the next world.

- Animals suffer, but Christianity does not see animals going to Heaven – what is the purpose, then, of this suffering?

Critical comments

'Life after death is possible, but we have seen no decisive philosophical reason for believing in it. Many religious believers would say that there are other reasons for belief in life after death. According to them, we can be sure that people survive death because survival after death is an item of faith.' (Brian Davies, *An Introduction to the Philosophy of Religion*, 1993)

'Many people today find the very idea of resurrection absurd, and it must be admitted that the physics of resurrection raises some fascinating difficulties. Let me mention the oldest philosophical objection ever raised against resurrection. Virtually all the Church fathers who discussed resurrection tried to answer it. What if a Christian dies at sea and his body is eaten by various sea creatures who then scatter to the oceans of the world? How can God possibly reconstruct that body? Or what if another Christian is eaten by cannibals so that the material of her body becomes the material of their bodies? And suppose God later wants to raise all of them, both the Christian and the cannibals. Who gets which bodily particles? How does God decide?' (Stephen T. Davis, 'Survival of Death', in *A Companion to the Philosophy of Religion*, 1997)

5.3: Revelation – Experience and scripture

For the exam you need to know about:

- The concept of religious experience.
- Consideration of visions, voices, 'numinous' experience.
- The concept of revelation through holy scripture.
- The view that scripture is divinely inspired.

Introduction

- Revelation means God revealing himself to people. For some, God's presence is revealed through God's handiwork (the design argument), but in this form the revelation is of an event that seems to have direct meaning and/or breaks natural laws. It conveys knowledge of God.

- Examples could include God speaking to Moses through the burning bush or the Angel Jibril speaking the Qur'an to the Prophet Muhammad (pbuh). Experience of God implies a direct sensory experience.

Visions, voices and the 'numinous' experience

- St Teresa of Avila had intense and extraordinary experiences of 'heavenly communications' including a 'mystical marriage', the 'espousal' of her soul to the person of Christ. She also had bodily manifestations of her spiritual elevation.

- Rudolph Otto (*The Idea of the Holy*, 1936) uses the word 'numinous' to mean being in the presence of an awesome power. Religion comes from a being separate from the world.

- The numinous is the holy, the ineffable core of religion. Experience of it cannot be described in terms of other experiences. Those who have a numinous experience sense dependency on an external force greater than themselves.

- Otto describes it as, 'The deepest and most fundamental element in all strong and sincerely felt religious emotion.' It is found in personal piety, rites and liturgies, religious buildings and monuments. It may be peaceful or fast moving and even violent. It can cause intoxication, frenzy and ecstasy.

- Visions and voices seem to break natural laws. Saul heard God speaking to him when he fell from his horse. Moses heard a voice within the burning bush speak to him.

- Visions may be seen, such as the three visitors who came to Abraham. In Western society today, talk of visions and voices draws scepticism from most people.

Conversion experience

- This means a change to a religious way of life because of some experience of divine truth directly or indirectly, such as St Paul's road to Damascus experience or Siddhartha Gotama's (the Buddha's) enlightenment experience under the Bodhi Tree.

- In the mind of the person, there is a transformation and a single aim or priority replaces all others. Religious aims become central to the person's life.

- William James (*The Varieties of Religious Experience*, 1902) believed it was necessary for religious ideas to form 'the habitual centre of his personal energy' and it could be triggered by explosive emotions.

- Conversion involves a recognition that the current lifestyle is wrong or incomplete and a change to lifestyle to bring about a better way.

- Sudden conversion may not be permanent but gradual conversion is more likely to be permanent.

- Conversion may be seen in intellectual terms or moral terms as coming to a new point of view.

- E.D. Starbuck (*The Psychology of Religion*, 1899) said conversion may be conscious and volitional (voluntary) and is a gradual process, or involuntary (self-surrender), which may be more sudden and which we finally surrender to.

- William James argued that some people could never be converted due to cynicism or strong atheistic beliefs and that this was a weakness.

Corporate religious experience and the 'Toronto Blessing'

- Usually, religious experiences are private, but there are cases when groups of people are involved. Corporate religious experience is public.

- An individual might see God or God's action in a public place or object. Such an event might involve a breach in natural law, such as Jesus walking on water or the coming of the Holy Spirit at Pentecost.

- Pastor Randy Clark encountered Howard-Browne in Tulsa, Oklahoma, and came under his influence. Clark was preaching at Toronto Airport Vineyard Church on 20 January 1994. Following the sermon, people began to laugh hysterically, cry, leap, dance, and even roar. This is seen as a result of the move of the Holy Spirit.

- The 'move of the Holy Spirit' has not stopped. Over the years, tens of thousands of people have flown to Toronto to participate. Afterwards, many people often become zealous and spread the activities to other places. The 'Toronto Blessing' has spread to evangelical congregations around the world.

Discussions

- Some see conversion as part of adolescent identity crisis as it tends to happen during that period. It could be a way of reorganising cognitive structures, seeing problems from a different perspective. However, there are cases of adult conversion.

- A psychological criticism of conversion came from Freud (1928), who considers it as a way of revitalising the ego through a positive internalised love object. Some suggest that people who have conversion experiences had prior childhood problems.

- Visions and voices can sometimes be explained through the use of hallucinogenic drugs, such as LSD. Some religions used hallucinogens to induce states of religious experience. Does this mean the experience would not be God? Can corporate experiences be explained as group hysteria?

- Religious experiences are subjective and not testable by empirical means. Even group witness statements are not necessarily a solid basis for evidence. Nevertheless, if religious people are prepared to change their life and take a more challenging course of action, they clearly believe their experience to be of divine origin. Many things we say are true cannot be tested or proven, such as whether a painting is beautiful, that a mother genuinely loves her baby rather than acting as if she does, for example.

- There may be neurological or physiological explanations of visions, or voices linked to medical conditions, or drugs. Believers argue God reveals himself in nature and through actions that do not break the laws of nature but are seen to have meaning: scientific explanations do not exclude God.

- It could be argued that genuinely-felt religious experiences make positive spiritual contributions to life.

Names and works

William James, *The Varieties of Religious Experience* (1902)

Rudolph Otto, *The Idea of the Holy* (1936)

Revelation through holy scripture

- For many believers of many religions, sacred scripture reveals something of the divine and the divine will. Most religions have sacred writings, though some, such as Hinduism, do not have a central single text.

- Disagreement emerges in the interpretation of scripture, how it is understood to reveal God. Some believers interpret scripture literally. This is true of most Muslims and many Christians, for example. The truth expressed is understood to be 'true' in an actual historical direct meaning.

- For Muslims, the Arabic Qur'an is the only real Qur'an as Allah revealed the Qur'an to the Prophet Muhammad (pbuh) in Arabic. Translations carry the meaning only. Orthodox Jews may interpret the Torah literally, while reform and liberal Jews might interpret the message for modern times.

- Many Christians argue that scripture is divinely inspired. That is to say, the words were written by a human but God, in some way, spoke through those words. Some suggest every word was intended by God. More liberal Christians may argue that the general meaning is God's intention, not every word.

- There are tensions between literal interpretations and knowledge of science, such as with the case of the miracles of the Hebrew scriptures and the New Testament, as well as matters of morality.

- Liberal religious believers often interpret their holy scriptures as divinely inspired but with cultural and historical influences that are relevant to the time of writing and not the present. The authors' own influence may also be responsible for some texts.

- Literalists criticise liberals for picking and choosing their interpretation. Liberal Christians might accept the story of the resurrection but not Jesus walking on water. Literalist Christians might argue that this picking and choosing is arbitrary and subjective.

Tips for A2 exam questions

'Revelation through scripture is more reliable than revelation through religious experience.' Discuss.

- You could either approach the question from the general arguments about religious experience or the argument for God's existence.

- You could investigate the validity of the evidence, exploring examples of specific religious experience.

- Arguments against from verification and psychology could be examined.

- Links with religious language could be explored.

Critical comments

'Of course, if there is a God who does appear directly or indirectly to individuals, then this is going to be either the timeless or the everlasting God. Interestingly, Nicholas Lash in his book *Easter in Ordinary* (1988), although affirming a creator God, rejects the possibility of this God appearing in any extraordinary way to human beings. Lash says that God is instead to be found in the ordinary things of life. If Lash is right – and I am not at all sure that he is – this places even greater weight on the individual's interpretation of his or her experience and hence, again, on his or her existing presuppositions. I am not convinced, therefore, that reports of religious experiences (to be contrasted with religious experiences which you or I may have personally) provide a sound foundation for faith.' (Peter Vardy, *The Puzzle of God*, 1990)

For the exam you
need to know about:

- The concept of miracle.
- Criticisms of miracle from Hume and Wiles.

5.4: Revelation – Miracle

The concept of miracle

- A miracle is held to be an action of God, or an invisible agent, which goes against the laws of nature and has some religious meaning or significance.

- Hume (*An Enquiry Concerning Human Understanding*, 1748) argues that nothing which can happen in nature can be classed as a miracle.

- Hick argues that as natural laws are made by observing what has happened, miracles are *a priori* impossible. When new things are observed, the understanding of natural law must be widened.

- Aquinas held that a miracle was something done by God which nature could not do, or could not do in that order, or is done in nature but without the usual operation of nature, for example, the sun going backwards, a person living after death, or an instantaneous cure of someone who may have been cured in time naturally.

- Swinburne (*Miracles*, 1989) gives examples of miracles as levitation, resurrection, water turning into wine. He notes that on its own a transgression of a natural law with no meaning is not considered a miracle.

- R.F. Holland ('The Miraculous,' in *Religions and Understanding*, 1967) notes that coincidences that do not break natural laws but have religious significance can sometimes be referred to as a miracle.

- However, striking coincidences happen all the time. Are they all miracles and, if not, how do you know which is which?

Criticisms of miracle made by Hume
An Enquiry Concerning Human Understanding (1748)

- Hume argues not that miracles do not happen but it would be impossible to prove one had happened. He says we must weigh the improbability of miracles against the evidence that they occur. Rational people will reject the evidence.

- Rationality requires that the belief is proportionate to the evidence. Evidence from the past supports the natural laws. Evidence suggests humans do not resurrect or walk on water.

- Witnesses who claim to have seen miracles cannot be given more credence than the absence of such miracles happening now. They are often less educated and may be fascinated by the fantastical nature of it so they suspend their reason.

- Hume suggests that different miracles in different religions cancel each other out. Since different religions have different claims to truth, you cannot have real miracles in all of them.

Responses to Hume

- C.D. Broad (1887–1971) notes that Hume assumes there are known fixed laws of nature, but science has observed exceptions to laws and on that basis revised the laws. Hume neglects the possibility that some of nature's laws are incorrectly understood.

- Hume does not address miracles he might witness, only the reports, which he discounts. Are all witness reports necessarily unreliable?

- Vardy (*The Puzzle of God*, 1990) notes that there is more evidence of miracles today than in Hume's time, such as the 74 attested miracles from Lourdes, which have been tested by objective scientists.

- Religions do not usually require people to believe on the basis of miracles. In the New Testament, faith came first and Jesus resisted the devil's attempt to tempt him to use miracles for his own aggrandisement.

- The statement that not enough people of significant education report miracles is problematic. How many exactly is 'enough' and what standing is enough? Who says that uneducated people are less truthful than educated ones; where is the evidence for that?

- In considering other religions, Hume suggests that different miracles in different religions are mutually exclusive and cancel each other out. Swinburne notes that evidence of a miracle in one religion might challenge the other but evidence of a miracle in another religion would mean there was evidence of miracles in both religions, or one could be true, and the other false.

- Is it acceptable to reject the evidence of others when it goes against what is probably the case? Thomas Sherlock notes that a person living in a warm climate where rivers never freeze might disbelieve reports from a cold climate where they do on the same basis.

Criticisms of miracle made by Maurice Wiles
God's Action in the World (1986)

• God never intervenes for individual acts, 'the primary usage for the idea of divine action should be in relation to the world as a whole rather than to particular occurrences within it.'

• The existence of individual divine acts is problematic. Why are they so rare? Why did they not occur when terrible things happened such as the atomic bombing of Hiroshima or the massacre of Jews in the Holocaust?

• An interventionist God is a weak idea of God. If God acts in the world, it raises all the issues of the problem of evil. God would seem to be arbitrary: allowing some suffering and evil to occur despite showing the possibility of divine intervention in particular cases elsewhere.

• It is better to conceive of God as having made the world as a single creative act rather than having to keep making small changes here and there.

Christianity and miracles

• For some believers, their religion is proved by signs and miracles, evidence of God's power and work.

• The Roman Catholic Church upholds the possibility of miracles and supports the literal interpretation of miracles in the Bible.

• Mark's Gospel suggests miracles do not come to make people believe but as a result of their faith.

• Literalist Christians hold that the stories of miracles must be taken as described and point to a divine ruler of the universe.

• Others give symbolic or metaphorical meaning to the stories – there is no breaking of any natural laws.

Tips for A2 exam questions

'Stories about miracles are an obstacle to faith for modern people.' Discuss.

• Explore the criticisms of Hume and Wiles and whether the concept of miracle is valid for modern people.

• Consider the argument that miracle stories support faith by demonstrating the nature and power of God.

• Consider the argument that miracle stories should be 'demythologised' to enable modern people to have faith without attempting to suspend their rational disbelief.

Names and works

David Hume, *An Enquiry Concerning Human Understanding* (1748)

Maurice Wiles, *God's Action in the World* (1986)

Critical comments

'A source of serious puzzlement has been that if spectacular miracles like the splitting of the Sea of Reeds, which was witnessed by over a million people and lasted for several hours, are to be believed, why is it that for centuries nothing comparable has been recorded as having happened? It may be noted that this problem constitutes part of the pressure of theists to renounce their belief that such fantastic events are genuinely historical. And, indeed, in the last hundred years or so, the denial of miracles has not been universally regarded as incompatible with theistic belief. No less a person than the Anglican bishop of Birmingham said that "miracles as they are narrated [in the scriptures] cannot in the light of our modern knowledge of the uniformity of nature, be accepted as historical".' (George N. Schlesinger, 'Miracles,' in *A Companion to Philosophy of Religion*, 1997)

5.5: Religious language

For the exam you need to know about:

- The *via negativa* (Apophatic way).

- The verification and falsification principles.

- The uses of symbol, analogy and myth to express human understanding of God.

The *via negativa* (Apophatic way)

- 'Apophatic' comes from the Greek word 'apophasis', which means 'negation'. It argues that God cannot be known in terms of human categories. God is beyond all signs and language. The great Jewish scholar Maimonides wrote that we come nearer to knowledge of God through negative attributes, for example, God is not limited, and so on.

- Arguably, speaking about God in negative terms avoids the problem of misrepresenting God.

Verification

- Logical positivism, developed from the Vienna Circle (a group of philosophers), looks at how we can verify knowledge empirically.

- The only propositions that are knowable are those which are analytic – *a priori* (through logical reasoning, without using external empirical evidence) and those which are synthetic (*a posteriori*) (which can be proved true or false (verified) through empirical experiment).

- The verification principle states that we know the meaning of a proposition if we know the conditions under which the proposition is true or false. Anything that cannot be measured analytically or empirically is meaningless. Talk of God, art and ethics are in this meaningless category for logical empiricists.

- A.J. Ayer, the British logical positivist, argued that propositions of science are meaningful as they are based on experimentation, but religious language is meaningless. Strong verification means there is no doubt about a statement; for example, 'The squirrel is red.'

- Weak verification means there are some observations that indicate truth, such as those about historical events that cannot be experienced now; for example, 'Julius Caesar was murdered.' However, the statements made by logical positivism cannot be proved by its own criteria analytically or synthetically.

- Hick argues that at the point of death we will have evidence of God's existence as we will perceive God. God will be shown to exist to those who already thought God did exist. He calls this 'eschatological verification'.

- Weak verification supports the claim that God is creator, with evidence from the design argument.

Falsification

- Anthony Flew argues that religious statements have no facts that can be proved true of false. An assertion must be subject to change if proved invalid and yet religious assertions can have no evidence placed before them and so cannot change. Therefore they are not valid assertions.

- Richard Swinburne argues that we can still derive meaning from unverifiable statements, for example, 'The toys come out of the cupboard when we are not looking.' We still understand what this statement means, even though we cannot verify it.

- R.M. Hare argues that religious propositions are non-cognitive but have meaning because they affect how people view the world, such as the student who believed his teachers were plotting to kill him, despite no evidence to prove it. His behaviour was affected.

- It can be argued that believers have a prior commitment to faith in God and do not allow evidence to undermine it.

Symbol

- Metaphors and symbols help bring understanding about God. Paul Tillich (1886–1965) believes they communicate religious experiences. Arguably, symbol and metaphor are closer to poetry, more mythical and evocative of the experience. Symbols go beyond the external world and open up levels of reality and depths to our soul. They participate in the greater reality.

- Some might argue, though, that symbols do not relate to factual information and are meaningless as they cannot be verified or falsified. Symbols cannot give insight to things beyond human knowledge. They cannot be tested for accuracy. Symbols relate to the real world, not beyond it.

- Paul Ricoeur (*The Metaphorical Process*, 1975) argues that 'the function of language is to articulate our experience of the world, to give form to this experience.' Through language we communicate our experience to others, forming new ways to conceive the world.

- Rather than suspending reality, for Ricoeur, a metaphor creates a new way of 'seeing' or constructing reality and opening new understandings of God that are impossible to communicate by the literal use of language.

Analogy

- How can language about the physical world be used to describe God?

- Aquinas rejected the claim that religious language could be univocal. Human love, in time and space, is not the same as God's love, which is beyond both.

- Aquinas also said religious language cannot be equivocal. The words cannot mean entirely different things. If there was no link between the two meanings, then we could know nothing about God.

- Aquinas looked to analogy. He used this comparison: the animal is healthy and the animal's urine is healthy.

- The health of urine and animal are different but they are connected as the animal produced the urine. God created the world and it depends on God, so when we talk of God's goodness there is a connection between it and the goodness of a human being.

- To say, 'God is good' is analogy of attribution. God is the cause of the goodness that a person has.

- Aquinas uses the example of the sun. The effects of the sun are similar to those of God. This example shows the remote resemblance between language about God's creation and language about God. You would learn very little about the sun by studying a tree.

- Another analogy is analogy of proportion: 'I know what a perfect circle is, so when you say God is perfect, I have a notion of perfection.'

- With both forms of analogy we are able to use language about God but cannot fully understand the meaning of this language.

- Ian Ramsey extends analogy. He talks about models and qualifiers. In 'God is good', 'good' is the model that we have a human understanding about. We add the word 'infinitely' (a qualifier) to 'good' so we can think in greater depth and get closer to an understanding of God's goodness.

Names and works

Thomas Aquinas, *Summa Theologica* (1273)

Anthony Flew, 'Theology and Falsification,' in *New Essays in Philosophical Theology* (1955)

R.M. Hare, in *New Essays in Philosophical Theology* (1955)

Richard Swinburne, *From Metaphor to Anaology* (1992)

Paul Tillich, in *Systematic Theology*, Vol. 1 (1951)

Discussions

- Problems in gaining knowledge about the attributes of God do not necessarily imply God does not exist, nor do they support the possibility of God's existence.

- People talking about God do not normally want to talk about God in terms of negation. Believers describe God in positive terms and in personal terms, rejecting the *via negativa*.

- Symbols and metaphors can give more imaginative understandings of God but could be too subjective to be of value. Metaphorical talk can be challenged by literal understandings. People can say, 'Is God really like that?' out of a desire for a literal understanding.

- God talk can be understood as having a truth embedded in myth. Rudolf Bultmann, in his essay 'New Testament and Mythology' (*Kerygma and Myth*, 1953), argued that theology must strip away to get at the truth. However, whether it is as easy to decide what is the mythological language that should be stripped away, as Bultmann suggests, is questionable. In any case, it is arguable that mythological language itself holds meaning.

Tips for A2 exam questions

'Speaking of God using symbol and analogy creates more problems than it resolves.' Discuss.

- You could explore philosophers' use of symbol and analogy, referring to Tillich for symbol and Aquinas for analogy, though any modern writers you have studied for this could also be explored.

- You could consider whether symbol touches the imagination more satisfactorily than analogy; whether it offers new insights or subjective views.

- You could consider whether the use of symbol and analogy are only of use for believers.

- Symbol and analogy may be culturally determined, so you might want to argue they can be misleading – the symbol of God as a shepherd does not convey as much in an urban society as in a traditional rural one, for example. There are the feminist issues of symbol and analogy being often anthropocentric, with perhaps the need for more feminised symbols to be included.

Critical comments

'It is not just a matter of saying that there must be some grounds for ascribing perfections to God. We must also insist that if we ascribe the same terms to God and creatures, then there must be a connection between the relevant criteria of evidence and truth. Thus the grounds for ascribing terms like "love", "father", "exist" and "life" must bear some relationship to the grounds used for our normal everyday application of these terms. Similarly, even if "God created the world" expressed a unique relationship, its truth conditions must bear some resemblance to our familiar uses of terms like "make" or "depends on" (which is not to say that we must expect to be able to verify the doctrine of creation empirically here and now).' (Patrick Sherry, 'Analogy Today,' *Philosophy*, 51, 1976)

6.1: Free will and determinism

Hard determinism

- Hard determinism maintains that we are not free and cannot be held morally responsible for our actions: 'All our choices, decisions, intentions, other mental events, and our actions are no more than effects of other equally necessitated events.' (Honderich)

- Predestination is a Christian view held by some Protestants that God has already decided who will be saved and who will not, suggesting that humans are not free to secure salvation. John Calvin (1506–64) described it as 'the eternal decree of God, by which God determined what God wished to make of every man. For God does not create everyone in the same condition, but ordains eternal life for some and eternal damnation for others.' (*Institutes*, 1559)

- Augustine (*Divine Election*, 4th–5th century) implied that God has some role in our formation as good or bad people: 'The potter has authority over the clay from the same lump to make one vessel for honour and another for contempt.'

- All actions have a prior cause. This challenges the notion of moral responsibility as people do not have freedom to deliberate or make a free choice.

- The sense of deliberation is an illusion. Spinoza wrote: 'Men think themselves free on account of this alone, that they are conscious of their actions and ignorant of the causes of them' (*Ethica Ordine Geometrico Demonstrata*, 1674).

- Traditional understandings of the scientific world and modern understandings of genetic engineering suggests there may be causal relationships or strong influences between one action and another action.

- Determinism means that we are mistaken to praise some people for being good or for blaming others for being bad as determinism calls the idea of moral responsibility into question.

- Determinism has been used in criminal cases as a justification for a lesser punishment when it demonstrated that the accused was not in full control of themselves (such

[handwritten margin notes: "Calvinist theological determinism", "philosophical determinism", "credibility of psychological determinism"]

as diminished responsibility when an abused wife murders her abuser husband).

- The upbringing of a person (nurture) can affect their ability to make moral decisions, though this does not necessarily mean they should not be punished.

- Some argue that determinism undermines moral responsibility and the possibility for using words like 'moral' or 'immoral'. Kant said, 'ought implies can,' defining moral actions as freely undertaken actions. If we are not free to act, we are not morally responsible for the act.

Soft determinism

- Some acts are determined, but we have some moral responsibility for our actions.

- Determinism does not rule out free will – the two are compatible and so moral decisions and moral debate remains possible.

- Some of our actions are conditioned, while others have so complex a collection of causes that they may properly be described as freely decided or willed.

- Soft determinists are criticised by hard determinists for failing to realise the extent to which human freedom is limited, and by libertarians for failing to realise the degree of human freedom that exists.

- Soft determinism offers an agreeable account of moral freedom as moral responsibility, and judgement is possible.

- Soft determinists have not agreed on precisely what is and what is not a determining factor in human action.

Libertarianism

- According to libertarianism, we are free and morally responsible for our actions.

- Human beings believe that they have self-determination or freedom to act: 'By liberty, then, we can only mean a power of acting or not acting, according to the determinations of the will; that is, if we choose to remain at rest, we may; if we choose to move, we also may.' (David Hume, *An Enquiry Concerning Human Understanding*, 1748)

- 'Man chooses not of necessity but freely.' (Aquinas, *Summa Theologica*, 1273)

Names and works

Thomas Aquinas, *Summa Theologica* (1273)

Augustine, *Divine Election* (4th–5th century)

John Calvin, *Institutes* (1559)

David Hume, *An Enquiry Concerning Human Understanding* (1748)

Benedict Spinoza, *Ethica Ordine Geometrico Demonstrata* (*Ethics Demonstrated with Geometrical Order*) (1674)

Glossary

Liberty Freedom.

Moral responsibility Our blameworthiness or praiseworthiness for actions.

- Moral actions are not chance or random events but result from the values and character of the moral agent.

- Humans have a sense of decision-making or deliberation and some give in to temptation, while others hold out.

- Libertarianism rejects cause and effect as a reason for human action but does not offer an alternative explanation for human action. It does not account for a human motive, which has cause of some sort.

Tips for A2 exam questions

'Unless we assume that everyone is free to make moral choices, we have no right to punish criminals.' Discuss.

- You could explore the implications of the idea of freedom of moral choice for moral responsibility, with reference to libertarianism and possibly Kant.

- You might explain how determinism implies a lack of moral freedom as criminals might be predetermined to offend because of nurture or nature (genetic disposition or upbringing). Examples should be given to illustrate this idea.

- If behaviour is inevitable and beyond the control of the criminal, should they be blamed or punished? Should good behaviour be praised or rewarded?

- The arguments of soft determinists could be included to contrast with hard determinists.

- Would it be possible for society to operate without a legal system and the presumption of some degree of moral freedom, even if it is only apparent and not actual?

Libertarianism – for moral responsibility = we have moral freedom to make moral choices –

Critical comments

Benedict Spinoza (*Ethica Ordine Geometrico Demonstrata*, 1674) notes that people are aware of their free action: 'An infant thinks it freely seeks milk, an angry child thinks that it freely desires vengeance, or a timid child thinks it freely chooses flight. Again, a drunken man thinks that he speaks by the free decision of the mind those things which, if he were sober, he would keep to himself...So experience teaches as clearly as reason that men think themselves free on account of this alone, that they are conscious of their actions and ignorant of the causes of them.'

A.J. Ayer (*Philosophical Essays*, 1959) argues that actions are either determined or not: 'Either it is an accident that I choose to act as I do or it is not. If it is an accident, then it is merely a matter of chance that I did not choose otherwise; and if it is merely a matter of chance that I did not choose otherwise, it is surely irrational to hold me morally responsible for choosing as I did. But if it is not an accident that I choose to do one thing rather than another, then presumably there is some causal explanation of my choice: and in that case we are led back to determinism.'

6.2: Conscience

For the exam you need to know about:

- The nature and role of the conscience.
- The views of Aquinas, Butler and Freud.

Conscience and Aquinas

- Aquinas believed conscience is the power of reason, a device or faculty for distinguishing right from wrong actions rather than an inner knowledge of right and wrong.

- People basically tend towards good and away from evil. Conscience is 'reason making right decisions'. (*Summa Theologica*, 1273)

- When making a moral decision, synderesis is right reason, an awareness of the moral principle to do good and avoid evil, and conscientia distinguishes between right and wrong and makes the moral decision.

Conscience and Joseph Butler (1692–1752)

- Butler stated that conscience is intuitive and a powerful moral authority, the final decision-maker.

- 'There is a principle of reflection in men by which they distinguish between approval and disapproval of their own actions…this principle in man…is conscience.' (Butler, *Fifteen Sermons*, 1726)

- Humans are influenced by two basic principles: self-love and the love of others. Conscience directs us towards focusing on the happiness of others and away from focusing on ourselves.

- Conscience determines and judges the right/wrongness of actions without introspection.

- Butler said, 'Had it strength as it had right, had it power as it had manifest authority, it would absolutely govern the world.' Conscience is 'our natural guide, the guide assigned us by the Author of our nature.'

Conscience and Freud

- Sigmund Freud saw conscience as guilt (*The Outline of Psychoanalysis*, 1938). The human psyche is inspired by powerful instinctive desires that have to be satisfied.

- Children learn that the world restricts these desires. Humans create the ego, which takes account of the realities of the world and society. A 'superego' internalises and reflects anger and disapproval of others.

- A guilty conscience is created, which grows into a life and power of its own, irrespective of the rational thought and reflection of the individual.

- The mature and healthy conscience is the ego's reflection on the best way of achieving integrity. The immature conscience (the superego) is a mass of feelings of guilt.

- The psychological account of conscience can undermine both Aquinas and Butler.

Newman and Piaget

- Cardinal Newman wrote: 'Conscience is a law of the mind…a messenger of him, who, both in nature and in grace, speaks to us behind a veil, and teaches and rules us by his representatives.'

- Following conscience was following divine law. Conscience is God speaking to us and has ultimate authority: 'I toast the Pope, but I toast conscience first.'

- You must do what you sincerely believe to be right and are justified in doing so even if you are mistaken.

- However, tensions between individual conscience and moral absolutes can occur.

- Piaget argues in *The Awakening* (1974) that there is a distinction between the conscience's deliberation of a moral rule and the practice of that rule. In effect, the practice is the effective moral behaviour and it is difficult to know at what point conscience coincides with practice.

Issues

- Conscience may be a moral source found within the human being, like the soul, which is distinctively human and provides a source for guilt and sense of moral obligation. Such an approach is challenged by Freud who argues that the external world forms the internal.

- Conscience could be a capacity that may be developed through moral education, but, on the other hand, may be left underdeveloped, leaving a person amoral and insensitive towards moral factors in life. This might be compatible with Freudian interpretations of conscience.

- Conscience could be a divine faculty that connects the person to the divine laws intuitively or through reason, though atheists would naturally dispute this possibility.

- Conscience may not be useful in ethics as we cannot measure what someone else's conscience is telling them, so conscience is difficult to evaluate.

- We may manipulate our conscience to justify our actions. Aquinas notes that it may be misled or misinformed, which could explain this.

- If conscience is the voice of God, how do we account for situations where conscience conflicts? Butler gives conscience ultimate authority, but some people commit horrific crimes which they justify by their conscience.

- People may not listen to their conscience correctly and may not inform their conscience, and so make mistakes.

- Conscience may not provide clear-cut moral guidance where there are conflicting obligations or duties, but instead may be more of a process or reasoned judgement.

- It is reasonable to consider conscience as part of the moral decision-making process. People can act with integrity and in accordance to ethical principles important to them.

- The judgement of those who break the law because of conscience must be moderated between those who seem to act for accepted ethical principles, while nevertheless breaking the law, and those who break fundamental ethical principles.

Tips for A2 exam questions

To what extent is conscience a reliable guide in sexual ethics?

- You should choose a particular topic from sexual ethics, such as homosexuality, to discuss.

- The tension between trusting conscience to act with integrity against the difficulty of acting impartially in matters of a sexual nature.

- There should be a discussion of Aquinas' comments about the possible weaknesses of conscience and the danger of ignorance as perhaps illustrated when conscience advises people to go against established moral laws.

- Consideration should be given to whether other moral sources should be used, such as moral laws/teachings, of the situation, and consequences of actions.

Names and works

Thomas Aquinas, *Summa Theologica* (1273)

Augustine, *De Trinitate* (400–16)

Joseph Butler, *Fifteen Sermons* (1726)

Sigmund Freud, *The Outline of Psychoanalysis* (1938)

Glossary

Conscientia The part that distinguishes between right and wrong and makes the moral decision.

Ego Created by humans, the ego takes account of the realities of the world and society. A 'superego' internalises and reflects anger and disapproval of others.

Synderesis Right reason; an awareness of the moral principle to do good and avoid evil.

- There could be some discussion of the term 'reliable' – how can we tell whether we are really being driven by our conscience or whether that 'voice' is coming from our parents' teaching, or our own will, or an outmoded religious stance, and so on?

Assess critically the nature and role of the conscience in ethical decision-making.

- Explore the different views of conscience, as well as psychological views.

- You could make an evaluation of ethical decision-making in relation to conscience, perhaps with an example.

- You could consider the limitations of conscience when informed by ignorance, as could the possibility of developing or refining it, and the dangers of guilt or the desire to satisfy others overriding reason.

- You might like to consider whether conscience alone is a satisfactory moral authority – what about the law, religious teachings?

- You could look at the reliability of conscience and factors that could undermine it.

- Give examples in your discussion illustrating the different moral dimension of action, including consequences, situations, intentions, as well as psychological, cultural and scientific influences.

Critical comments

Henry David Thoreau (1817–62) (*On the Duty of Civil Disobedience*, 1849) argued for the ultimate supremacy of conscience over the law: 'After all, the practical reason why, when the power is once in the hands of the people, a majority are permitted, and for a long period to continue, to rule is not because they are most likely to be in the right, nor because this seems fairest to the minority, but because they are physically the strongest. But a government in which the majority rule in all cases can not be based on justice, even as far as men understand it. Can there not be a government in which the majorities do not virtually decide right and wrong, but conscience? Which majorities decide only those questions to which the rule of expediency is applicable? Must the citizen ever for a moment, or in the least degree, resign his conscience to the legislator? Why has every man a conscience then? I think that we should be men first, and subjects afterwards. It is not desirable to cultivate a respect for the law, so much as for the right. The only obligation which I have a right to assume is to do at any time what I think right.'

6.3: Christian ethics

For the exam you need to know about:

- The main ethical precepts of any one religion.

- The purpose of ethical behaviour in any one religion.

- The contribution made by any one religion to practical ethical issues.

- The nature of the ethics of any one religion in comparison with other systems.

- This book has chosen Christianity for this part of the exam. You may be doing a different religion. This book also considers different denominations of Christianity. This is not required by the OCR course.

Sources of Roman Catholic ethics

- There are diverse approaches to Christian ethics according to the denomination.

- Roman Catholic ethics are based in part on Aquinas' Natural Law and in part on Virtue Ethics.

- Natural Law is a key ethical theory underpinning Roman Catholic Christianity with its emphasis on reason as a tool to perceive Natural Law and its deontological emphasis in the application of the primary precepts. Some acts are intrinsically right or wrong, good or evil in themselves.

- Conscience also plays a role for Roman Catholic ethics with Aquinas' view that conscience is reason, making moral decisions that must be informed by prayer and worship, the teaching of the Church, experience, and the inner voice of the Holy Spirit.

- The Roman Catholic Church also refers to Virtue Ethics: Aristotle's idea that our moral actions determine the nature of our character and Aquinas' idea that we must practise the virtues to make good behaviour habitual.

- Sacred scripture is an important source of ethical guidance in Roman Catholic Christianity, which cannot be changed. The Ten Commandments, the Sermon on the Mount, and other key texts about Christian discipleship and behaviour form what is known as 'divine positive law', which no human can change.

- The role of the person is important as well as the acts themselves.

Protestant Christian ethics

- There are different approaches to ethics amongst Protestant churches.

- Reinhold Niebuhr (1892–1971) applies the Gospel to social issues through love: 'The primary issue is to derive a social ethics from the absolute ethic of the Gospel…social ethics must be concerned with the establishment of tolerable harmonies of life, tolerable forms of justice.'

- Paul Ramsey (*Basic Christian Ethics*, 1950) sees Christian ethics as 'obedient love' or 'love fulfilling the law'. Analysing ethical problems from the viewpoint of Christian love simply means that Jesus Christ is the centre.

- Joseph Fletcher (*Situation Ethics*, 1966) sees ethics as depending on the situation rather than any deontological basis, and argues that the person should seek the most loving outcome.

- More conservative Protestants offer an absolutist interpretation of Christian ethics. Robertson McQuilkin (*An Introduction to Biblical Ethics*, 1995) sees the Bible as a revelation by God of God's will for human nature and that universal Bible norms are absolute.

- Lewis B. Smedes (*Mere Mortality*, 1987) focuses on the commandments, fulfilled by the coming of Jesus, as embodying an enduring human law.

- There is a sharp divide between those who take a deontological approach to moral norms espoused in the Bible and those who focus on Jesus' love as a power that overcomes the constraints of laws.

- Protestant Christians have different views on current issues such as abortion and homosexuality. Evangelical Christians prohibit abortion and homosexual sex as acts that contravene biblical laws, while more liberal Christians have exceptions through the application of love.

The purpose of ethical behaviour

- For most Christian Churches, ethical behaviour comes from a sense of obedience to God and a desire to live life in the way that God advocates.

- Christian discipleship is the attempt to live in a way that imitates Christ and in doing so helps to bring about the Kingdom of God.

- Many Christians also see moral behaviour as behaving in a way that suits the human being. God has made humans and gives advice on how they can live life to the full.

- There is also a fundamental sense in which moral behaviour enables the Christian to enter into God's kingdom or Heaven, though in itself good acts are not the critical factor. More important are acts of repentance and a desire to do good.

Names and works

Thomas Aquinas, *Summa Theologica* (1273)

Aristotle, *Nicomachean Ethics* (4th century BCE)

Joseph Fletcher, *Situation Ethics* (1966)

Alasdair MacIntyre, *After Virtue* (1981)

Robertson McQuilkin, *An Introduction to Biblical Ethics* (1995)

Paul Ramsey, *Basic Christian Ethics* (1950)

Lewis B. Smedes, *Mere Morality* (1987)

Glossary

Bible norms Biblical moral rules.

Deontological Ethics that focus on acts which are intrinsically right or wrong.

Situationism Fletcher's theory, which seeks for loving outcomes from a given situation.

Virtue Character traits for moral education.

Christian ethics: deontological or teleological?

- Most Christian ethics are deontological with Catholics often seeing acts as intrinsically right or wrong according to their compatibility with Natural Law, and, along with many other Christians, a sense of obedience to the divine law reflected in the biblical ethical teachings.

- More radical is the Situationist approach, which is both teleological, as it pursues a most loving outcome, and relative, as it considers each situation separately with no idea that actions are right or wrong in themselves.

- Some liberal strands of Roman Catholic ethics are personalist with an emphasis on putting the person at the centre of the moral equation rather than the act or the consequence.

- There is also the Virtue Ethics dimension, based on Aristotle, which sees the improvement of human character in terms of living a more Christ-like life. Here, the focus is on becoming more fully human.

- Virtue Ethics is a source of Roman Catholic ethics – our moral actions determine the nature of our character and there are desirable virtues to cultivate within.

Tips for A2 exam questions

To what extent is the religion you have studied consistent with a Utilitarian approach to ethics?

- You could start by outlining the general situation that religious ethics tends to be focused on acts, while Utilitarianism is focused on ends.

- You might consider how religious ethics (with examples from Natural Law or divine command sources, perhaps) contrasts with Utilitarianism, which applies a principle that evaluates the options, looking for the best possible results.

- You could explore the consequences of these differences: that Utilitarianism might be prepared to break commonly agreed rules, sacrificing an individual for a greater good, while many religious ethical systems would not allow rules to be abandoned in this way.

- You might consider the exception of Situationism, which seems to cross the barriers, and Fletcher's justification that Situationism is a religious ethic.

- While happiness or pleasure is a core idea of Utilitarianism, love or compassion is a far more important idea in some religious ethics. Consider the case that love can be sought in the way Situationism claims.

Critical comments

Reinhold Niebuhr (*An Interpretation of Christian Ethics*, 1935) writes: 'I still believe, as I have believed then, that love may be the motive of social action but that justice must be the instrument of love in the world in which self-interest is bound to defy the canons of love at every level…The primary issue is to derive a social ethics from the absolute ethic of the Gospel. The Gospel ethic is absolute because it merely presents the final law of human freedom: the love of God and the neighbour. A social ethics must be concerned with the establishment of tolerable harmonies of life, tolerable forms of justice.'

Robertson McQuilkin (*An Introduction to Biblical Ethics*, 1995) sees the Bible as 'a revelation by God of his will for human nature…Those laws or other teachings that derive from, interpret, or reinforce one of the Ten Commandments should thus be recognised as having enduring authority.'

6.4: Environmental ethics

For the exam you need to know about:

• Practical ethics, ethical theory, and religious ethics as applied to environmental ethics.

What is environmental ethics?

• 'Environmental ethics' includes the preservation of species, the conservation of habitats, the depletion of biodiversity and natural resources, the ozone layer, and the effects of pollution.

• It is concerned with our attitudes towards and impact on the biological and geological dimensions of the planet, how that affects humanity, and the well-being and diversity of other forms of life on earth and geological systems.

• There are concerns among many scientists that human activity is unsustainable and will harm the future well-being of human life, that of other forms of life on earth, and will damage permanently the earth's geological systems.

• A few challenge this view arguing that development protects us from the environment and enables us to counter the extremes of weather and failures of crops.

Criticism of religious approaches to environmental ethics

• The Judaeo-Christian Bible is accused of encouraging human domination and exploitation of the world: 'Let them have dominion over the fish of the sea, and over the fowl of the air.' (Genesis 1.26) Thomas Aquinas maintained that 'all animals are naturally subject to man'.

• Some philosophers criticise the Judaeo-Christian tradition for placing humans at the moral centre and leaving the environment as morally insignificant (an anthropocentric view).

• Genesis makes humans dominant over the world and humans are encouraged to multiply over it and subdue it – the natural world exists for the benefit of humans and nature has no intrinsic value.

• Revised beliefs and values could be proposed that emphasise the responsibility humans have for the earth, prioritise the improvement in the quality of life over material production, and to use material resources carefully and protect the quality of the environment.

Defence of religious approaches to environmental ethics

- Religious ethics are often theocentric (God-centred) as God is the underlying reason for moral behaviour. This includes environmental ethics. They are also anthropocentric in that Christian/agape love of neighbour is the fundamental principle for human relations as the environment affects the quality and ease of human life, and geo/biocentric in that creation is 'God-made' and good and therefore must be preserved because it is a good in itself.

- The environment is God's sacred creation. Humans are stewards, responsible to God for their use of the world God has made. Humans are *created* and their activity has worth as part of God's creative process. Technology and science are not intrinsically bad. God works in and through nature and it is important to God (see Psalm 19).

- Pope John Paul II writes that environmental damage has come about because humans have set themselves in place of God and tyrannised nature, ignoring God's purpose for it.

- Christians can be called to reject lifestyles that disregard and damage God's creation, that force the poor into greater poverty, and that threaten the right of future generations to a healthy environment.

- Creation has value in itself and reveals God. Christianity teaches that human acts should reflect God's own love for creation as human life depends on it. Sin distorts the human relationship with the natural world, damaging the balance of nature. A Christian's relationship with God is affected by how he or she uses creation's gifts.

- 'What is wrong is a style of life which is presumed to be better when it is directed towards having rather than being and which wants to have more, not in order to be more but in order to spend life in enjoyment as an end in itself.' (Pope John Paul II)

- Humans must observe environmental justice, which means the impact of their lifestyles on others and the world. The desire for affluence and greater wealth can dominate.

Deep ecology and some criticism

- Deep ecology is an attempt to define a secular environmental ethic that recognises value in all life forms, the natural systems and diversity of earth, and rejects anthropocentric ethics.

- Leopold (*Round River*, 1949) called for a new ethic dealing with humans' relation to land and the animals and plants that grow upon it. He sought to enlarge the boundary of the moral community to include soils, waters, plants and animals, or collectively the land.

- Leopold says: 'A thing is right when it tends to preserve the integrity, stability and beauty of the biotic community. It is wrong when it tends otherwise.'

- Arne Naess and George Sessions ('Basic Principles of Deep Ecology,' *Ecophilosophy*, Vol. 6, 1984) proposed that all life was intrinsically valuable, irrespective of its usefulness. They argued that deep ecology sought to 'preserve the integrity of the biosphere for its own sake', not for any possible human benefits.

- Some extend this to include natural objects or systems, arguing that all organisms and entities in the ecosphere, as parts of the interrelated whole, are equal in intrinsic worth.

- J. Lovelock's hypothesis sees the ecosystem as an entity that must be considered in any moral deliberation (*Gaia: A New Look at Life on Earth*, 1979).

- Singer (*Practical Ethics*, 1993) maintains that while life forms can have value as part of the diverse interrelated geophysiological structure of the planet, only sentient life has intrinsic value. Other organisms cannot truly be said to desire to flourish or have experiences.

- Singer believes Lovelock's use of the Greek Goddess Gaia to describe the world confers on the earth a consciousness which is not there.

Names and works

Thomas Aquinas, *Summa Theologica* (1273)

Aldo Leopold, *Round River* (1949)

James Lovelock, *Gaia: A New Look at Life on Earth* (1979)

Arne Naess and George Sessions, 'Basic Principles of Deep Ecology,' *Ecophilosophy*, Vol. 6 (1984)

Peter Singer, *Practical Ethics* (1993)

Glossary

Anthropocentric Centred on humans or human interests.

Deep ecology An environmental ethic that sees the natural world as having intrinsic value in itself.

Theocentric An environmental ethic centred on God and God's creation.

Tips for A2 exam questions

How far would you agree that environmental issues are more of a concern to a religious believer than to a Utilitarian?

- You could consider the potentially destructive ends that misuse of the environment might lead to and how a Utilitarian should react, as Utilitarians should consider the greater good.

- You may also consider that a religious believer may feel very protective of what s/he sees as a divinely created world, which must be protected as it is.

- Alternatively, you could explore the idea that the believer sees the world as created for him/her to use, with no concern to allow the natural world to be protected for any other reason than service to humanity.

- You might also explore the idea that a Utilitarian would only see the world as a resource for humankind and not consider any natural feature as anything other than a resource.

- These different arguments could be considered in relation to the arguments from religious environmentalists, deep ecologists and the other arguments discussed above.

Critical comments

Kakadu National Park, in Australia's Northern Territory, contains rugged woodlands, swamps and waterways, supporting a rich variety of life. It contains species found nowhere else, such as the hooded parrot and the pig-nosed turtle, which are endangered. Kakadu affords aesthetic enjoyment and recreational and research opportunities. Many think it is a place of immense beauty and ecological significance. It is of spiritual significance to the Jawoyn aboriginals. Kakadu is also rich in gold, platinum, palladium and uranium, which some think should be mined. If this happens, then, environmentalists claim, aesthetic, recreational and research opportunities will be reduced, the beauty of Kakadu will be lessened, species will disappear, ecological richness will decrease, the naturalness of the place will be compromised and the spiritual values of the Jawoyn discounted. Mining already goes on in the Kakadu area and there is pressure to allow more. Should more mining be allowed? Should any mining at all be allowed? (Robert Elliot, 'Environmental Ethics,' in *A Companion to Ethics*, 1997)

6.5: Sex and relationships

For the exam you need to know about:
- Practical ethics, ethical theory, and religious ethics as applied to sex and relationships.

Christian approaches to sexuality

- Early Christians saw celibacy as a holy state. Jesus' second coming was believed to be imminent, bringing with it the end of the world, so marriage and reproduction were no longer thought necessary. Also, Jesus did not marry and St Paul recommended celibacy for all who could withstand the temptations of the flesh. The Roman Catholic Church requires celibacy for its priests. Most other Christian denominations do not.

- Most Christian Churches envisage sex as a practice exclusively for those committed in permanent loving relationships. Sex outside marriage, adultery, masturbation, and homosexual sex may be seen as sinful either because of biblical statements or Natural Law ethics.

- Genesis relates sex to having children. Natural Law sees reproduction as the only purpose of sex and contraception is forbidden for preventing God's purpose.

- Christianity traditionally identified the purpose of marriage as fidelity to one another, procreation and union of the parties. Recently, a greater emphasis has been given to the uniting element of marriage. The Anglican Church has said that 'the commitment is made in love for love'.

- Jack Dominion (*Passionate and Compassionate Love*, 1991) believes that a new definition or description of sex is needed; one that sees sex as a personal expression that communicates recognition and appreciation, confirms sexual identity, brings reconciliation and healing, celebrates life, and is a profound way of thanking each other for the loving partnership that they have.

Other approaches to sexuality

- Contemporary presentations of sex emphasise a libertarian and contractarian ethic – sex is morally permissible if there is mutual agreement or consent between the participating parties. Sex is not linked with marriage or reproduction. Freedom and autonomy preside.

- Libertarians may adopt the harm principle and observe that no harm is done to either party or other third parties: 'My freedom must not restrict another's or harm them.'

Adulterous sex harms the betrayed spouse, so the act is wrong.

- This view celebrates sexual liberation embracing freedom and endorses a more tolerant and permissive attitude towards women, homosexuals and sex outside marriage generally.

- Feminists criticise both the traditional Christian approaches to sexuality and the liberal ones. Christian approaches rest on a defined cultural role for women, that of the child bearer, wife and submissive. This disempowers women, restricting their status in society and socialising them to meet the desires of men.

- The Hebrew and Greek view of women has meant that for centuries they have had little access to politics, wealth and very little free choice. Sexual behaviour assumes male dominance and female submission – most sexual crimes are committed against women.

- Liberal approaches to sexuality are criticised by feminists because these approaches assume a level playing field between the sexes. Feminists argue that women may not be as free as men to enter sexual relationships due to their oppression by men.

- The feminist Catharine Mackinnon (*Feminism Unmodified: Discourses on Life and Law*, 1987) argues that sexuality must be re-imagined and remade before moral sexual relationships are possible. Until this is done, sexual activity is immoral.

Christianity and homosexuality

- There is a growing belief that there is no moral issue about same-sex relationships beyond the issues that apply to heterosexual relationships, and yet prejudice against homosexuals exists, as seen in the nail bombing of a gay bar in London's Soho district.

- Homosexual acts were once crimes in the UK and homosexuality was considered a mental illness. In medieval times, homosexuals were burnt at the stake.

- Christianity has traditionally seen homosexuality as wrong because there is no possibility of life from the act (Natural Law), because it is outside marriage (only sex in marriage is permissible), and because of specific Bible passages, which imply a divine prohibition.

- Biblical texts are used as a basis for the condemnation of homosexuality: 'You shall not lie with a man as with a woman: that is an abomination' (Leviticus 18.22), and it is punishable by death (Leviticus 20.13). St Paul describes people engaging in same-sex sexual acts as 'dishonouring their bodies', and his statement is often cited to justify condemnation of gay relationships.

- The worldwide Anglican community stated that the ordinations of 'practising homosexuals and the blessing of same-sex unions call into question the authority of holy scripture'.

- Critics of this approach do not accept that scripture can be interpreted and applied in this way. Other rules from similar texts are not enforced in the same way. So Gareth Moore (*The Body in Context: Sex and Catholicism*, 1992), for example, writes that if some Christians arbitrarily follow the law in Leviticus, which says it is immoral for a man to lie with a man, they are still unlikely to follow the passage later on that advocates beheading as punishment or Leviticus 19.19, which forbids the wearing of garments made of two kinds of material.

- The Roman Catholic Church maintains there is no sin involved in an inclination towards a member of the same sex. The homosexual person should be treated with respect, compassion and sensitivity, and not discriminated against. They are called to chastity. Homosexual acts themselves are sinful, depraved and intrinsically disordered.

- Critics of the Natural Law approach to homosexuality argue that sex has a non-reproductive purpose, the uniting act between a loving couple. Most sexual acts cannot lead to pregnancy, such as sex in the non-fertile part of the monthly cycle, sex after the menopause, sex when one or both partners are infertile, or sex when the woman is already pregnant. If the reproductive imperative in sex is rejected, then Natural Law no longer opposes homosexual sex.

- Sexual organs are suited for reproduction and the production of intense pleasure in oneself and others. To condemn people for using their sexual organs for their own pleasure reveals the prejudices and taboos of our society.

- Liberal Christian writers maintain that the quality of the relationship, be it heterosexual or homosexual, is what determines its moral value. They dispute the interpretation of biblical passages and draw on the teaching that all are made 'in the image and likeness of God'. God created homosexual men and women, so they must be good. A good God could not intentionally create disordered human beings.

- Gareth Moore argues that there is a Christian basis for an inclusive attitude towards homosexuals because it is a religion that positively seeks to make room for the marginalised, outcasts and failures in society.

Tips for A2 exam questions

'Absolute moral rules have no place in personal relationships.' Discuss.

- Are personal relationships so individual that general universal principles cannot be applied?

- Does the application of deontological absolutist rules cause harm to people's unique relationships?

- Consider whether there are any principles or some categorical imperatives that are binding in every relationship. For example, is adultery wrong if no one involved is hurt or concerned about it?

- Should homosexual relationships be condemned if no one is harmed and some people find fulfilment through them?

- Ethical theory and its point of view should be applied, be it Utilitarian, Natural Law, Kantian, Situation Ethics or Virtue Ethics, to support your discussion.

How effective is Natural Law when applied to an issue of sexual ethics?

- You could explain that Natural Law ethics is deontological and expresses primary precepts, which all actions must be measured against.

- The priority of reproduction in sexual matters could be explained and you could give the examples of how that is interpreted by the Roman Catholic Church in relation to contraception, homosexuality, masturbation.

- You could consider whether there is a single human nature with regard to sexuality.

- You could look at the idea of a purpose for human sexual organs and the impact that it has on sexual ethics issues such as masturbation and homosexuality.

- You could discuss whether matters of sexual ethics can have deontological laws applied and, if so, which these might be and whether they might be incompatible with certain lifestyles.

- You could explore whether the precepts that Natural Law traditionally outlines need to be refined or rejected or whether the theory in itself provides a corrective to modern-day excesses.

Critical comments

'We are convinced that homosexuality and lesbianism are clearly a deviation from the natural norm and divine order and those who practise homosexuality and lesbianism are in sin (Romans 1.24–7)…Some Westerners have introduced homosexual practices in the Great Lakes Region of Africa, but we, as Africans, repudiate the practice and do not wish it to be seen in our Province. We want to promote stable, monogamous marriage between a man and a woman within the love of God.' (Statement on homosexuality by the Anglican Province of Rwanda, 31 January 1998, http://newark.rutgers.edu/~lcrew/rwanda.html)

Desmond Tutu, the Anglican Archbishop of South Africa, wrote on homophobia: 'We reject them [homosexuals], treat them as pariahs, and push them outside our church communities, and thereby we negate the consequences of their baptism and ours. We make them doubt that they are the children of God, and this must be nearly the ultimate blasphemy. We blame them for something that is becoming increasingly clear they can do little about.' (February 1996, www.religioustolerance.org/hom_ang2.htm)

6.6: War, peace and justice

For the exam you need to know about:

- Practical ethics, ethical theory, and religious ethics as applied to war, peace and justice.

Holy wars

- Wars against the Muslim control of Jerusalem in the Middle Ages were seen as holy wars or crusades, some churchmen saw the First World War as a war for the Kingdom of God.

- A holy war is guided by God but Christian Churches have rejected this idea.

- Islam has a concept called 'jihad' (the Arabic for 'fight', or 'conflict'), which is a personal individual struggle against evil in the way of Allah. It can also be a collective defence of a Muslim community.

- Most modern theologians reject holy war as it expresses a simplistic view of God that supports one particular national interest and rejects mercy for the enemy.

Just War

- Just War theory explains when it is right to fight and how war should be fought. It was explained by Thomas Aquinas.

- The Old Testament portrays God as leading the Hebrews to victory in battle and St Paul argues that rulers are servants of God when they execute God's wrath on domestic wrongdoers.

- Just authority means war started by a legitimate authority. Wars cannot be started by private citizens or incompetent governments.

- Wars should be fought for a just cause, which means those who are attacked should deserve it. The just cause might be to protect innocent life, or guaranteeing basic human rights, for example. The intention should be just, which means for the advancement of good or the avoidance of evil.

- During the conflict, right intention means pursuit of peace and reconciliation including the avoidance of unnecessarily destructive acts or imposing unreasonable conditions.

- There has to be proportionality between the injustice that led to the war and the damage done by war in terms of suffering and loss of human life. The damage to be inflicted and the costs incurred by war must be proportionate to the good expected by taking up arms.

- War must be the last resort with all peaceful attempts at resolution exhausted before violence. There should be a fair chance that the war will be won. Hopeless suffering and loss of life for no constructive purpose is wrong.

- There should be comparative justice, so both sides to the conflict must be fairly considered.

- There are rules of conduct in Just War theory, although such rules have often been ignored in practice.

- International agreements, such as the Geneva and Hague Conventions, seek to limit certain kinds of warfare. Senior Serb commanders were successfully tried for war crimes in the war in Bosnia.

- Christianity has advocated conditions of conduct to limit destruction and who may be killed. Only the minimal force necessary should be used and non-combatants should not be killed.

- Just War theory attempts to maintain core moral principles in a framework to permit the use of violence in controlled circumstances and against certain targets.

- It does not allow wanton acts of violence in the national interest but only the use of minimal force, and seeks to preserve basic human rights and take account of justice.

- Realists argue that the Just War conditions are ambiguous or too simplistic. Wars are caused by complex reasons, there may not be a single 'just' cause. Outcomes of war are difficult to calculate and it is not always clear that peace will be the result or that success is likely. To expect fighting soldiers who have to kill their opponents to keep their thoughts free from malice or prejudice towards those opponents is implausible.

- It is unclear who is a 'just target' in war. A soldier is a combatant, but a civilian population supporting the army through industrial activity is also supporting the war machinery.

Pacifism

- Pacifists argue that Just War theory ignores Jesus' rejection of violence to prevent his capture and also his advocation of love of enemies.

- Pacifists argue that war is always wrong. In its most extreme form, pacifism is the opposition to all forms of violence as a means of settling disputes, either between individuals or between countries, including self-defence.

Names and works

Thomas Aquinas, *Summa Theologica* (1273)

Reinhold Niebuhr, *Moral Man and Immoral Society* (1932)

Glossary

Jihad Muslim concept of a personal individual struggle against evil in the way of Allah, which can also be a collective defence of the Muslim community.

Pacifism The idea that violence in war, and possibly individual matters as well, is wrong.

Proportionality Using appropriate measure of force that the situation demands and not causing excessively destructive consequences.

Realism The view that different moral rules apply in the defence of a community.

- Siddhartha Gotama, the founder of Buddhism, required that his followers renounce violence.

- Early Christians refused to fight in the Roman Imperial army, interpreting pacifism from Jesus' teachings about loving our neighbours as ourselves, turning the other cheek, and from his order to Peter to drop his sword.

- Several Reformation churches are pacifist, including Moravians, the Society of Friends (Quakers), and the Church of the Brethren. Members refuse to bear arms and fight.

- Some are pacifists for philosophical reasons, believing that killing or physically attacking another human is intrinsically wrong, and the loss of life, human suffering and tremendous economic, social and moral damage caused by war is too great.

- Pacifism is difficult to maintain, especially as it takes away from the victim the right to judge whether a violent response is just (self-defence).

- The widespread use of mass deportations, and even mass exterminations, shows the weakness of pacifist principles.

Realism

- Some Christians, such as Reinhold Niebuhr, rejected pacifism for 'Christian realism'.

- Realism considers human nature to be evil, so human communities must use force to maintain a just and ordered society.

- The usual moral rules that restrict harming or killing each other do not apply to communities or states that have special rights necessitated by their status.

- A war that serves the national interest is morally acceptable.

- Christian realists see pacifism as a heresy, which assumes that love is guaranteed victory over the world. Pacifists expect God's will to prevail without realising they have a duty to be proactive in the world. They do not recognise that God rules through human institutions such as governments and the courts.

- Some might question the special rights that national governments are granted by realism, arguing that there is no moral difference just because a number are gathered together.

- Pacifism places limitations on individual rights of self-defence, which, given the existence in the world of weapons of mass destruction and the practice of genocide, appear unacceptable.

- Realism provides no limitations to a government's actions in war and in an era where there are war crimes against large civilian populations. Arguably, there should be some limitations on governments in war.

Tips for A2 exam questions

Discuss how ethical theories might be applied to issues of war and peace.

- You could consider the application of deontological ethical theories to killing, such as whether Kant would group warfare in the same terms as murder, or whether the Natural Law precept to protect life means not killing or defending with lethal force those in danger of being unjustly killed. You could consider whether both could advocate pacifism based on a 'kingdom of ends' (Kant) and preserving life.

- You could explore the teleological theories of Utilitarianism and Situationism and how they might provide a more pragmatic approach than absolute pacifism, or a justification for war if the consequences merited it.

- Contrast the pacifist argument with the Just War theory that war in certain circumstance may be justified if fought in a certain way – consider the Second World War in this light.

- The weaknesses of any ethical justification of war could be illustrated through other conflicts of contested morality, such as a the second Iraq War, the Falklands War, or the Vietnam War.

Critical comments

'We utterly deny...all outward wars and strife and fighting with outward weapons for any end or under any...pretence whatsoever; this is our testimony to the whole world...The Spirit of Christ by which we are guided is not changeable, so as once to command...us from a thing of evil and again to move us into it; and we certainly know and testify to...the world that the Spirit of Christ which leads us into all truth will never move us to...fight and war against any man with outward weapons, neither for the Kingdom of Christ nor...for the kingdoms of this world...therefore we cannot learn war anymore.' (Excerpts from a statement made by the Religious Society of Friends to King Charles II, 1660)

'I...told them I knew from whence all wars arose...and that I lived in the virtue of that life...and power that took away the occasion of all wars; and that I was come into the covenant...of peace which was before all wars and strife.' (George Fox, founder of the Religious Society of Friends, 1650)

Part 7: Synoptic Paper A2: Connections in Religious Studies

Answering synoptic questions

Answers to the synoptic questions are marked at the same standard as the rest of the A2 papers. You are not expected to be more knowledgeable and intelligent in the synoptic section. The marks are divided in the same way for knowledge and understanding and evaluative skills. The important thing is to answer the question specifically rather than trying to include everything you have done on the related topics. You do not have to try and divide what you say between philosophy material and ethics material as long as you address the question.

7.1: Conscience and the moral argument; conscience or the sense of moral responsibility as possible evidence for the existence of God

- This topic links the work you have done on conscience in ethics with the work you have done on the moral argument for the existence of God and the criticisms of it in philosophy.

- People have a concept of conscience linked to their sense of moral responsibility and guilt. It is considered important to act with integrity in accordance with what a person believes to be right. That belief is informed by their conscience.

- Aquinas, Butler and Newman all argue that conscience exists and is informed by God, be it understood as a rational tool for discerning the Natural Law or an intuitive way of hearing the 'voice of God'.

- Conscience seems to indicate the existence of morality. We have a clear notion of having done the right thing or not. Sometimes we feel obliged to do the thing we do not want to do, out of a sense of moral obligation, even if it will not be easy and may harm us.

- Conscience implies some sort of moral authority, a guiding principle or objective voice.

- Newman argues that conscience suggests the existence of God. Adams conceives rightness as in accordance with God's will. If God does not exist, there is no morality.

- The sense of moral obligation informed by conscience is evidence supporting Kant's contention that human beings discern the moral law.

- Moral people act out of obedience to this moral voice. Kant argues that in a perfect world moral behaviour should lead to happiness, but as this does not always happen, Heaven must exist as a place where this is the case, implying that God exists.

- God's existence is morally necessary and conscience is evidence supporting the argument.

Arguments against conscience as possible evidence for the existence of God

- Freud provides a non-religious argument for conscience, identifying it as the superego, the internalised parent that conveys disapproval when we act in a way that contravenes our parents' morals. It may be more mature and is the name for a sense of moral integrity. It could be argued that God uses the human psyche as a way of conveying morals in this mature sense.

- Arguments against a religious interpretation of conscience undermine its use as evidence of God. Consciences seem to vary, suggesting that if God exists and works through conscience, God is arbitrary or that, in fact, conscience is not connected with a divine objective moral code but personal emotions.

- Conscience is used to justify actions that others consider immoral. Conscience may be able to be manipulated. This tends to suggest it is not evidence of God's existence.

- Even if conscience is informed by God, it is not empirically testable and could not be used as evidence to support the moral argument if the person had no sense of morality. However, many people do have a sense of right and wrong.

- Those who already accept the existence of an objective right and wrong may be inclined to believe there is a God and those who believe in God already may accept conscience as evidence of that fact. However, many atheists do have a belief in morality and would be unlikely to accept conscience as evidence for the moral argument.

7.2: The concept of free will and determinism in relation to the nature of an omniscient God

- This topic links the work you have done on hard and soft determinism and libertarianism with philosophical ideas about the nature of God.

- Does an omniscient God remove the possibility of human freedom?

- If God created us and knows every aspect of our genes and personalities, if God has created the people around us who influence us, and when God created us, if God knew all the choices that would ever confront us and what we would choose, are we acting freely when we make our moral choices? If God knows the future actions of every person, in what sense are humans free?

- The God of classical theism is considered to be omniscient (all-knowing). A God that is not all-knowing might seem unworthy of worship or status.

- If God is all-knowing, is human action affectively predetermined or predestined? Some Christians argue that God has already decided who will receive eternal punishment and who will receive eternal damnation.

- Determinism holds that humans are not free. All acts are necessitated by prior causes and any sense of true freedom is false.

- This raises a number of questions. Why would God create automatons and then punish them for the sins they committed by his or her design? Would sin exist in a meaningful sense as the person had not willed to go against God but simply followed his or her design?

- Many philosophers argue that moral responsibility is only possible with free will and that humans have freedom to act.

- Libertarianism is the belief that people are free to act and morally culpable for their actions.

- People have a sense of freedom. They have a sense of moral deliberation when deciding what to do. They feel temptation, which they may give in to or resist.

- Some argue that while humans are affected in part by the physical bodies that they have, when it comes to morality, they are free.

- If humans are in fact free, then how can God be truly omniscient? If God has foreknowledge of our actions, then are we free? Some argue that God's foreknowledge does not take the freedom away.

- A parent who knows their child may have strong reasons for thinking that the child will abuse a freedom the child requests, yet at the same time, the parent may feel he/she must afford the child the freedom they request, even if they then watch the child making the very mistake they expected. The freedom of the child is real just as the parent's foreknowledge is reliable.

Issues of the extent to which God can be held to know the future, and the implications of this for human responsibility

- Some argue that God is limited to knowledge of the present and past but is not in a position to know the future acts of individuals. Traditionally, some have argued that God is eternal and exists beyond time and space and knows all events in time, while others argue God is everlasting and exists within time and so does not perceive the future of that time in the same way.

- Traditionally, people are thought to be free to act and only morally responsible for those actions if they are free. Kant says that moral imperatives imply a possibility to do them, 'ought implies can'.

- Human freedom is a defining feature of what it is to be human and we have a sense of moral deliberation.

- Augustine argues that we are created free to turn our will to God but God knows, if God is all-knowing, the evil that we will do if we turn away. God could have chosen not to create those God knew would do evil.

- On the other hand, while God has knowledge of our future actions, God has not willed us to do them. We have free will to act in such a way and must, therefore, be responsible for those actions.

- Horrendous moral actions and sufferings might question whether God's decision to create was a moral one.

- Irenaeus argues that God has created humans imperfect to become perfect in life. Perhaps God is responsible because we were created with the capacity for wrongdoing and God has the future knowledge of the inevitability of sin and our individual sins.

- Alternatively, perhaps God does not have knowledge of the future, just knowledge of the past and the present, though this seems to limit God beyond that of classical theism.

- Plato suggests that it is possible for human beings to seek out the good. Aquinas believes humans tend to the good and Kant believes people have a sense of the moral law.

7.3: The relation between free will and the problem of evil

- Does evidence of human free will counter the challenge of the problem of evil?

- The problem of evil is how can there be a good God, all-powerful and all-knowing, when evil exists?

- According to Irenaeus, evil in the world is necessary to improve the souls of people. This implicates God in intentionally bringing about evil, which seems morally unjustifiable.

- According to Augustine, the presence of evil and suffering is a result of human action against the will of God. Swinburne argues that humans are necessarily given the capacity to do evil because they are free.

- Human beings seem to have free will to do good or bad and are morally responsible for those actions according to Aquinas and Hume.

- Humans have a sense of moral deliberation and we naturally blame people for doing bad things and praise people for doing good things.

- However, there is evidence that human freedom is limited. Some argue that there are genetic influences over human choices. Determinists argue that freedom is an illusion and all actions are the consequence of prior causes.

- If human action is determined by biological imperative, it is difficult to justify the human suffering in the world. Without the free will defence, God's act of creating can be challenged as irrational and immoral.

- Determinism does not simply undermine the free will defence but the classic nature of God or God's existence. A more limited first cause God might be conceivable, but not a God involved in the world today.

7.4: The implications for ethics of the theories of psychology and sociology

- This section brings together the work you have done on psychological and sociological challenges to religious belief and experience with the work you have done on moral relativism and the nature of conscience.

Is morality formed by the human mind rather than God?

- Freud sees religion as a collective neurosis built to prevent individuals falling into personal neurosis. It comes from an infantile desire to return to the bliss of the mother's breast.

- Religion offers a wish fulfilment to overcome the tension individuals have of living in society. Conscience and our sense of moral obligation comes from this tension. The superego is an internalised moral parent giving guilt to restrict our actions.

- On the other hand, Jung offers a psychological account that incorporates God. People have a collective unconscious in which there are archetypes, one of which creates religious images. This archetype is influenced by an external source. Moral ideas are related to this.

- While both psychologists provide psychological accounts for religion, they are each contested.

- Many believe there are certain moral laws that should not be broken and human moral behaviour could be seen as influenced by these socially perceived ideas. This does not mean that there is no God and no morality, for arguably, God works through psychology.

Is morality formed by society rather than God?

- It is the case that there are societal causes for the values that a community expresses, but that in itself does not mean morality is not linked to God. Some argue there are only the values expressed by society, while others argue there are objective values, which have a divine source.

- Marx argues that religion masks economic inequality by requiring adherence to a moral code and justifying the inequalities on earth in terms of heavenly justice, which will be received in the future.

- Durkheim argues that religious ideas and moral ideas are projections of the authority of society and that in the modern world we should replace the religious ideas with those of society.

- Morality enables a society to cohere, but that in itself does not mean morality is formed by society. Indeed, a society's values may be considered by some to be immoral, such as those enforced by the Nazi German government.

- There are some differences in moral codes between societies and cultural relativists argue this is evidence that there is no objective moral code. On the other hand, some philosophers argue that there are enough common principles.

Does sociology demonstrate that God has nothing to do with morality?

- It might be argued that, even if moral codes are formed by societies for different purposes, this does not rule out the possibility of God as an absolute standard or judge.

- Sociologists are concerned with the function of religion and morality for a society rather than with the existence or otherwise of God or absolute moral norms, although some, such as Marx, have tried to use sociological arguments to explain away the need for religious ethical codes.

7.5: The relation between ethical language and religious language

- The argument of logical positivism affects both the meaning of ethical and religious language.

- The only propositions that are knowable are those that are analytic and those that are synthetic. Facts are either observable or logically necessary. Moral and religious statements are neither and so are not meaningful according to logical positivism.

- The verification principle states that we know the meaning of a proposition if we know the conditions under which the proposition is true or false. Anything that cannot be measured analytically or empirically is meaningless. Talk of God and ethics are in this category.

- A.J. Ayer considers moral statements to be emotive expressions. Anthony Flew argues that religious statements have no facts that can be proved true or false, and the same can be said for ethical statements.

- Richard Swinburne argues that we can derive meaning from unverifiable statements, such as, 'The toys come out of the cupboard when we are not looking.' We know what this statement means even if it is unverifiable.

- R.M. Hare argues that religious propositions are non-cognitive but have meaning because they affect how people view the world. Religious people give symbolic or analogical meaning to language in understanding God and live according to those understandings.

7.6: The relation between moral behaviour and life after death

- Is it worth behaving morally if there is no life after death?

- Why be moral? There could be non-religious reasons for being moral based on the secular humanist approach.

- Kant argues that there is a duty to follow the divine law, as does Aquinas, though there is no guarantee that doing good leads to moral happiness in this world.

- If people are simply being good to get into Heaven, is this selfish? Are their motives pure? Not according to Kant, who argues one should act out of duty, not personal self-interest. Perhaps they need to have good motives in order to get to Heaven.

- It seems hard to justify the suffering that sometimes occurs for individuals being good, as a personal sacrifice, if they personally do not benefit in any way in the next world.

- The judgement of the wicked seems to justify the moral behaviour of the good.

- Hick's 'eschatological verification' for various claims made by religion can be considered.

- The universalist concept of life after death, in which all are forgiven and reconciled with God, might be considered to be a reason for not bothering to behave morally, as a person could enjoy a life of sin in the confidence of eventual forgiveness.

- In Eastern religious traditions, the point of behaving morally is to achieve good karma for the next life and ultimately an escape from endless rebirth. If you could not come back in a lower life and were guaranteed oblivion at the point of death, why be moral?